Heritage of Ireland

Brian de Breffny

ENDPAPERS *Landscape in Connemara.*

House Editor Esther Jagger
House Art Editor Allison Waterhouse
George Weidenfeld and Nicolson Ltd
91 Clapham High Street London SW4

ISBN 0 297 77675 4

Printed in Great Britain by
Butler & Tanner Ltd, Frome and London

Heritage
of
Ireland

Brian de Breffny

Photographs by George Mott

Weidenfeld and Nicolson London

Contents

Introduction

Ireland's cultural heritage forms a fascinating and complex tapestry. For thousands of years successive waves of incomers reached the shores of Ireland and made it their home, imposing on the resident population new social patterns, religious beliefs, and more sophisticated culture and technology. In time each of these immigrant groups integrated with the old inhabitants, embracing certain aspects of their way of life.

The primitive civilization of the Mesolithic hunters was absorbed by the Neolithic farmers. The Celts, in turn, overwhelmed the society which had built the great Megalithic monuments, although elements of the older culture persisted. When the Christian missionaries came to Ireland the inhabitants accepted the essentials of Christian doctrine, but the structure and codes of the pagan society continued and pre-Christian magic remained for many centuries. The Christian Church flourished for nearly 700 years in a form peculiar to Ireland. Even after the ecclesiastical reforms of the twelfth century, distinctive customs continued, but the influx of Continental monastic orders brought new disciplines, new styles and new practices to Ireland. The barbarous Vikings who swept down on the Irish eventually settled and founded the first towns, which soon became important trading ports. The inhabitants of the Norse kingdoms were converted to Christianity, adopted the language of the Irish and were assimilated. The cultural and social contribution of these Norse settlers has only emerged in recent years in the light of modern scholarship and recent archaeological finds.

When the Anglo-Normans thrust their way into Ireland they made radical changes in the legal system, enforced new social patterns, introduced technological improvements and altered the face of the countryside in the areas where they settled. Within three centuries, however, their descendants had been Hibernicized and had intermarried with the Irish and adopted their customs.

Because the fashions and philosophy of the Renaissance barely touched Ireland, the medieval life-style persisted; in the seventeenth century Ireland was the harbinger of a vanishing way of life. The Elizabethan and later the Cromwellian settlers from England, and the Scots settlers of the Jacobean Plantation of Ulster, were separated by their religion from most of the Irish population and were therefore less vulnerable to the cultural influences of their adopted country than previous incomers had been. Nevertheless, despite the religious and political differences and despite the stubborn colonial attitude of many of the settlers, Irish influences gradually filtered through to them. Separated from their ancestral culture and society by the Irish Sea, and enjoying a privileged position in Ireland, the descendants of the planters developed a life-style and traditions of their own, so that to the English living in England they seemed to be Irish, while to their Irish neighbours they appeared English. Some of the settler families took pains to avoid contact with the

Irish, basking in their own presumed superiority; but within a century of the Cromwellian settlement a large number of these settlers' descendants had inter-married with the Irish and adopted their customs. The influences were, however, mutual, and the determination of the settler community and of the administration to colonize inevitably resulted in widespread Anglicization of the Irish population. Eventually, from the dual society of Gaelic-Irish and British settlers, new trends emerged. In remote areas a dwindling population of Irish-speakers clung tenaciously to their own ways, shunning the alien presence, while the bulk of the population became more or less Anglicized. The consciousness of the minority of settlers who stayed aloof was barely penetrated by the Irish presence, while most of their descendants, the so-called Anglo-Irish, were to some degree Hibernicized.

The emergence of nationalism, and the birth of a literature and visual arts which found their inspiration in the ancient past, affected members of both societies in the nineteenth century. Out of it came a robust new artistic tradition in painting and sculpture and a wealth of distinguished drama, poetry and creative writing. It also forged a brand of Irishness with a rather spurious ancestry and character with which many of the inhabitants identified themselves, and by which they were identified by outsiders. This was the image of the devil-may-care, feckless, warm-hearted, improvident, lovable, drunken Irishman and the ravishingly beautiful, irresistibly charming and unassailably virginal Irish colleen. The repertoire of this tradition was an amusing, confusing mixture of ancient Irish heroes, firbolgs, saints and scholars, shamrocks, shillelaghs, leprechauns and piety. Meanwhile, in Ulster, the descendants of the Scots and English settlers nurtured a contrasting tradition with its own strange repertoire – King Willie on his horse, Union Jack sashes, biblical fundamentalism and black bowler hats. The Anglo-Irish gentry, too, seemed to live up to the stock image created for them of high-living, hunting, gambling, wenching, mortgages and haughty superiority, against a background of fine silver, good claret, family portraits and eccentric behaviour. The unfortunate generations who were weaned on the parochial attitudes of illiberal Protestantism or strict Roman Catholicism remained curiously isolated from the outside world and impervious to its outlook. The ramparts of this parochialism, in which religious fervour, political nationalism, patriotism, chauvinism and myth are inextricably mixed, have only been breached in the last decades, largely by the mass media (especially television), by the rapid increase in travel facilities available to a more affluent society, by the expansion of higher-level secular education, by the fresh breezes of ecumenism, and by increased cultural and commercial exchanges with other countries.

Heritage of Ireland looks at the various strands of the Irish cultural heritage against its historical background, and at the multi-cultural factors which have marked and fashioned the Irish scene, the Irish character and the national identity.

1 Prehistoric Ireland

*Ireland before the
arrival of man*

The oldest rocks in Ireland, at Rosslare and at Kilmore Quay in County
Wexford are, according to radio-metric determinations, not less than
2,000 million years old. These pre-Cambrian rocks emerged in the massive
rock-folding of the Caledonian upheaval, when a land mass rose from the sea
which stretched from Scandinavia to the Atlantic. About 350 million years ago that
land mass was almost submerged by a warm, tropical sea which flooded all but the
highest ground.

Another upheaval occurred some 80 million years later – the Armorican upheaval
raised the land mass and left what is now Ireland above the general level of the
flooding seas; 10 million years later, at the end of the Armorican upheaval,
Ireland's land mass was roughly sculpted.

In the Mesozoic Era, which began about 225 million years ago and lasted for
some 150 million years, reptiles dwelt in what is now Ireland. At this time it appears
that the sea and land levels oscillated, and it is likely that much of the country was
submerged under the cretaceous seas which left a mantle of chalk. In the course of
dramatic earth movements at the end of the era, when the Atlantic Ocean took its
shape and Greenland moved away from Europe, molten lava welled up and flowed
over the land, leaving it covered with dark basalt. Ranges such as the Mountains of
Mourne were created when the magma cooled and solidified into granite at a centre
of igneous activity.

The Cenozoic Era, which followed the Mesozoic, saw mammals in Ireland living
in a warm climate in which a dense tropical forest flourished, including such exotic
trees as the redwood, the swamp cypress and the black gum, as well as alder, lime,
oak and holly. Then about 25 million years ago the climate began to cool; there were
oscillations, but the general trend was downward. Specialization among the hitherto
undifferentiated mammals began at this time. Volcanic action and earth movements
continued until at least 17 million years ago. The cooling continued for some 4 million
years and the temperature grew so cold that ice caps formed at the North Pole;
Ireland's tropical forests vanished, to be replaced by a tundra of grasslands and open
vegetation.

By 2 million years ago the cold had become severe, and when the winter snows
overtook the summer thaw large masses of ice formed over Europe; about 200,000
years ago almost all of Ireland was buried beneath a thick covering of ice. The
protective mantle of clay was torn away by the ice, and many signs of its effect are
visible in the Irish landscape today; the most impressive perhaps are deep valleys
like the Gap of Dunloe in County Kerry. This famous beauty spot is in fact a great
glacial breach, where a tongue of ice gouged a gash 1,500 feet deep. Where the
discharge tunnels of sub-glacial streams silted up, eskers were left – long, sinuous

OPPOSITE *The Gap of Dunloe,
Killarney, County Kerry. A
glacial breach where a tongue of
ice gouged a gash 1,500 ft deep.*

FOLLOWING PAGES *The giant
deer. An artist's impression by
Charles R. Knight.*

ridges unrelated to the surrounding topography. Where masses of ice embedded in gravel melted and the overlying drift collapsed, kettle-holes were created; hollows developed where ice mounds melted and slumped. Deep gorges, now often stream-less, were carved out by the glacial meltwaters; where sand and gravel were discharged into a lake held in a valley by an ice dam a delta was formed; and moraines built up where gravel and blocks of rock were deposited at the margins of ice bodies. Where boulder clay was fashioned into ovoid masses under the ice sheet a landscape of drumlins was left when the ice disappeared – long whale-backed ridges usually parallel with the direction of the ice flow. Drumlin country can be seen in County Armagh, where the two cathedrals, Protestant and Roman Catholic, stand on neighbouring drumlin hills, in mid-Down, where drumlins dominate the landscape, and in County Mayo, where eighty or more little whale-back islets dot Clew Bay.

Geologists and geomorphologists are able to discern other less evident marks left by the ice sheet, such as the ice-wedge polygon patterns created by shrinkage cracks. In regions such as Clogher Head on the Dingle Peninsula of County Kerry there was evidently no ice cover: the Minnaunmore Rock with its serrated edge shows the results of solifluction from frost action, seemingly at the margin of the ice sheet, but reveals no signs of glacial action.

The last 100,000 years of the Cenozoic Era after the Ice Age were characterized by fluctuations in temperature. Inter-glacial warm periods occurred, and it was warm enough about 31000 BC for mammals to live in Ireland. There is evidence of the existence of the elephantine woolly mammoth, brown deer, spotted hyena, wolf, Arctic fox, giant deer, reindeer, hare and lemming. But these creatures failed to survive another cold period in about 24000 BC, when a major advance of ice covered all but a belt across the extreme south of Ireland and a few smaller areas, including the extreme north-west of Mayo and parts of Donegal. Some Arctic alpine plants managed, however, to survive: mountain avens, mountain sorrel and purple saxifrage, for example, survived in places not over-ridden by ice, and are still found today on Ben Bulben, County Sligo, and Slieve League, County Donegal.

Towards the end of the Cenozoic Era, and certainly between about 10000 BC and 9000 BC, the giant deer flourished in Ireland, feeding on the rich grasslands of what are now the counties of Down, Meath and Limerick. It was a magnificent creature; the male stood around 10 ft high to its antler tips, and the antlers, shed and regrown annually, grew to a span of about 10 ft and weighed up to 66 lbs. Reindeer also roamed the country, but in lesser numbers. When the thermometer plunged again about 8500 BC, and a 500-year period of cold ensued, the grasslands perished and the giant deer became extinct in western Europe. Man may also have existed in Ireland then, but the evidence is tenuous and controversial, resting on a single skeletal find in a cave in County Waterford. The remains did not permit accurate radio-carbon laboratory tests and there was no supporting evidence such as the presence of Early Stone Age implements, but chemical tests indicated that the bones might date from 9000 BC or earlier. If man did reach the ice-free southern belt of Ireland, however, he would not have survived the final 500-year spell of intense cold.

The warm stage in which we now live began about 8000 BC. The land bridges which joined Ireland to Britain had not then all disappeared and, until those high morainic ridges were drowned by the rising sea, plant and animal immigration was brisk. Even so, only about half the flowering plants from the Continent that reached Britain made it to Ireland; the Mediterranean strawberry tree reached the islets in Lough Gill, and an insect which could neither swim nor fly managed to emigrate from its home in Morocco or Portugal and travel along the Atlantic coast via Brittany and Cornwall to Ireland. Slow-moving reptiles did not arrive in time to make the crossing before the land bridges disappeared.

Shortly after the beginning of the warm stage, pine, hazel, elm, oak, willow, alder, juniper and birch had reached Ireland. Soon a vast woodland grew up, intersected by a network of streams and rivers in the lowland areas and interrupted by lakes. Beneath lay Ireland's mineral wealth and coal deposits, such as those near Arigna, County Roscommon and near Castlecomer, County Kilkenny.

Man settles in Ireland

The first human inhabitants to have left definite evidence of their presence arrived at about the time of the disappearance of the land bridges. They were very primitive people, unaware of the mineral wealth of their new habitat and interested only in the fish and birds they trapped. They used Microlithic implements, pointed flints and little axes made from flint flakes. The first evidence of the settlement of these people comes from Mount Sandel, above the River Bann, south of Coleraine in County Derry, and shows that they were there by 6600 BC. Where did the Mount Sandelites come from? Unfortunately not enough of their settlement was preserved to be able to identify them with other people of their time. From its location in the extreme north it would seem that they arrived via the short sea crossing from Scotland, and it is likely that their original home was Scandinavia. The fate of the Mount Sandelites – how or when the colony died out or left – is unknown.

At the north-west corner of Lough Neagh evidence has been found of another settlement, dating from round 6200 BC, and of the same immigrants at sites along the eastern coast of Antrim. Many thousands of their implements were found in the beach gravels at Larne, County Antrim, hence their name of Larnians. Like the Mount Sandelites, the Larnians belonged to a Mesolithic culture; they had no knowledge of agriculture and lived a semi-nomadic life, camping in the forest in small clearings laboriously made with chipped flint and stone implements. They lived by fowling and fishing and their diet included shellfish, water-lily seeds and hazel-nuts. The Larnians' origin is unknown, and there is not enough evidence from a residential site to be able to identify them with any contemporary group in another land. However, because of the location of their first settlements in Ireland, we can assume that they too came from south-western Scotland; their journey may have begun in Scandinavia since the floor of the present North Sea was then dry, permitting a land crossing from Denmark to the north of England. Unlike the Mount Sandelite colony, the Larnians had continuity; for about 3000 years, however, their descendants made scarcely any technical or cultural advancement, although they penetrated inland as far as the midland lakes and moved southward along the eastern seaboard. During those millennia Ireland seems to have attracted no other immigrants, and because of their inability to clear large areas of the primeval forest the Larnians changed the landscape little. Natural changes were taking place, though, and fens and marshes – the first step in the development of raised bog – were growing up and forming on the edges of the great lakes. The vegetable debris consolidated into fen peat as early as 7000 BC, as has been proved by radio-carbon testing on Ballyscullion Bog, County Antrim. As the fens extended, the adjacent lakes shrank, and where the vegetable debris accumulated faster than the rate of decay, bogs grew.

The Neolithic farmers

The vanguard of the next immigrant group, the first farmers, may have reached Ireland about 3600 BC. Early evidence of their presence comes from radio-carbon tests on charcoal from Neolithic sites at Ringneill Quay, County Down, where bones of domestic animals were found, and at Dalkey Island just off the Dublin coast, giving dates around 3400 and 3300 BC. Radio-carbon testing of charred timber planks from a Neolithic dwelling in a hilltop settlement at Ballynagilly, County Tyrone, shows that it was inhabited in 3200 BC, while a radio-carbon test on charcoal from a pit on the site surprisingly gave an earlier date of between 3700 and 3600 BC.

In comparison with the aborigines, the descendants of the Larnians whom they found when they arrived in Ireland, the newcomers were enormously sophisticated and technically advanced. Their own ancestors, who originated in the Middle East, had moved up through the Balkans about 5000 BC, bringing with them agricultural skills and the arts of pottery and stone-polishing. From south-eastern Europe these Neolithic farmers fanned out across the central European plains, and eventually reached north-west Europe. The groups that came to Ireland must have been well organized for a sea-crossing in primitive craft which had to transport families, livestock for breeding and seeds for the first crops of wheat and barley. Undoubtedly scouts were sent in advance, and the success of the immigration indicates that these people were not only ambitious and industrious but also capable of intelligent planning and gifted with qualities of leadership.

H.J. Case has concluded that the first farmers arrived in Ireland in curraghs, boats of the type still in use in the west of Ireland. With a helmsman and a crew of eight oarsmen a boat could have transported several adults and their children, or a bull and cow with a couple of calves and a few dogs, or half a dozen pigs, or about ten sheep or goats. The sea crossing had to be a short one because of the problem of watering the trussed-up livestock, so it is likely that they embarked in south-west Scotland or near Anglesey.

With their wooden-handled polished stone axes the Neolithic famers were able to make substantial clearings in the primeval forest to create grazing patches and tillage plots. They then erected a stockade to protect the compound from marauders, and fenced the cultivated tillage area to protect it from the grazing stock. The first farmers also erected timber dwellings. The house at Ballynagilly, County Tyrone, on a hillock with a good spring nearby, was a rectangular structure of planks, roughly 21 ft × 19 ft 6 ins with corner posts supporting its long sides, which were set in trenches; two post-holes in the centre of the house were probably for a roof-tree; there were two hearths. A Neolithic house excavated at Ballyglass, County Mayo, was also rectangular but this well-built dwelling had a supporting timber framework of posts set in holes. Post-built houses on a circular plan have been excavated on Slieve Breagh, County Meath.

The Neolithic axe was an amazingly efficient implement, capable of felling a hundred trees without breaking. In north-eastern County Antrim the settlers discovered outcrops of porcellanite, particularly suitable for axe-heads; they also found and used epidiorite, Mourne granite, dolerite, porphyry and other minerals, as well as flint. The Neolithic settlers' tools included adzes, chisels and scrapers as well as weapons such as arrowheads and kite-shaped javelin heads; they manufactured pottery vessels typified by an out-turned rim, and simple, useful artefacts such as baskets woven of alder rods and probably bound together with rushes. The most impressive example of the genius of the Neolithic farmers, however, was their extraordinary stone tombs. The aboriginal Mesolithic inhabitants gradually adopted the artefacts of the more advanced incomers and eventually, it seems, were assimilated into their world.

The court-grave builders

Differing burial practices in Neolithic Ireland indicate that immigrants with different cultural affinities, and therefore apparently from different places, arrived in Ireland after the first settlers. The custom of interment, in communal burial places or in single graves, was one clear group distinction, but even within the confines of these two cult practices the usages of different groups varied. The earliest kind of burial place was a stone mound over a long trapezoid stone burial chamber fronted by a semi-oval or semi-circular enclosed court – they are known as court-graves or court-cairns. Stone, flint and pottery artefacts found in the burial chambers were presumably the personal property of the deceased, placed there because these people believed in some kind of after-life. Animal bones found at court-grave sites appear to be the remains of funeral feasts. Over 300 court-graves have been found in

ABOVE *This large vessel from a Neolithic single grave at Linkardstown, County Carlow, was found in a cist with an adult skeleton, pottery shards and an axe-head.*

RIGHT *Creevykeel court-grave, County Sligo. Dating from the Late Stone Age, it is one of the finest examples in Ireland.*

Ireland, almost exclusively in the north, and scattered from the west coast to the east. The concentration in north-western Mayo and in Sligo and Donegal, as can be seen from the court-grave distribution map, suggests that parties of Neolithic settlers landed there from south-west Scotland, where court-graves are also found.

The passage-grave builders

Communal burial was also practised by the passage-grave builders, but their funeral cult entailed cremation; the dead were burned with personal ornaments such as bead necklaces of semi-precious stones, pendants simply carved in the shape of tools, chalk balls, and mushroom-shaped antler pins. These pins may have been hair-pins, but their phallic form and similarity to a stone phallus found at the Knowth passage-grave has been noticed by archaeologists Dr Herity and Dr Eogan. The pottery bowls found on the passage-grave sites usually have bevelled rims and stab-and-drag decoration of rough chevrons and loops; the type is known as Carrowkeel Ware.

As the distribution map of the Boyne-type passage-graves indicates, the immigrants who built them and who first arrived in Ireland around 2800 BC appear to have landed on the east coast of Ireland, and then pushed inland; it looks as though they came via Anglesey, through Wales and south-western England. There had been communities of passage-grave builders along the Atlantic seaboard of Portugal, concentrated along the present frontier of Portugal and Spain, and in Brittany. A connection between the Irish passage-grave people with those of Brittany is indicated by their probable route of arrival, supported by slight similarities in their method and style of tomb-building and decoration, although there is a time lapse of about 1,000 years between the Breton and Iberian passage-graves and those excavated in Ireland. The Irish passage-graves, usually on hilltops, consist of a long passage through an earth mound into a corbelled stone tomb chamber, which, in

The distribution of court-graves in Ireland and western Britain.

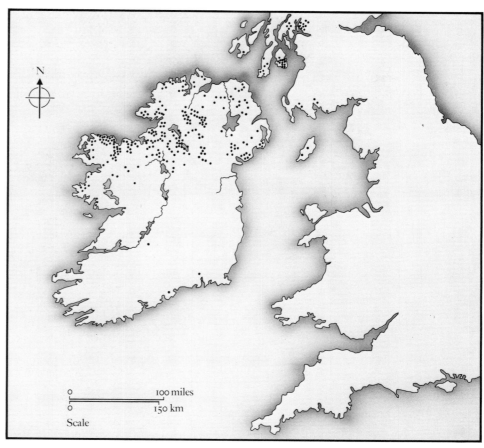

The distribution of passage-graves in Ireland and western Britain. (Both maps after Herity and Eogan.)

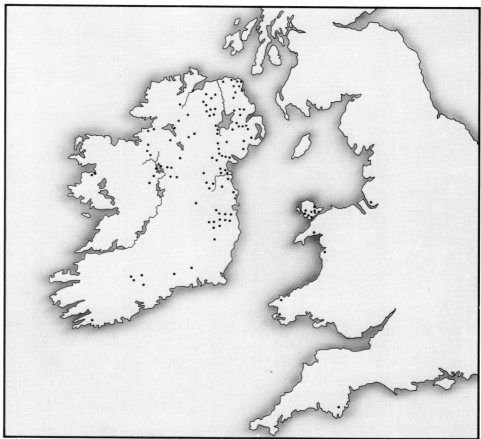

the case of an important burial place, was lofty and had a massive portal. Sometimes the main tomb mound was surrounded by a cluster of satellite mounds, each with its own passage and tomb chamber. At Knowth, one of three important passage-grave mausoleums on hilltops above the River Boyne, the enormous main burial mound, about 33 ft high, is almost 300 ft in diameter. Fascinating motifs were patiently picked out on stone, especially on the kerbstones encircling the tumulus, which were decorated in this manner with curvilinear and rectilinear designs. Spirals seem to have been the favourite motif, but there were also arcs, serpentiforms, zigzags and chevrons; the designs seem abstract but they may have had some esoteric cult significance which now escapes us. At Knowth archaeologists discovered a stone bowl, so decorated, which may have been used in funeral rites.

The extent of learning attained by the passage-grave builders was suddenly and amazingly revealed when Professor M.J.Kelly discovered in 1969 that a roof box over the tomb chamber at Newgrange, another Boyne valley mausoleum, was designed and arranged so that the sun entered the chamber only on midwinter day (21 December) and the days immediately preceding and following it. The fact that the builders of this passage-grave, around 2500 BC, wanted such a device, and that they were able to align the tomb and the roof box with the exact position on the horizon where the sun rises on the dawn of the winter solstice, demonstrates their knowledge of astronomy (a science which had been developed in Assyria and Babylon before 3000 BC) and their ability to follow through an intellectual process and realize it through their technical skill. A vast workforce would have been required to construct these mausoleums. Unless the passage-grave people arrived in great numbers they must have recruited their manpower among the indigenous Mesolithic and earlier Neolithic population.

A view of the main chamber of Newgrange, County Meath.

The portal-grave builders

In the late Neolithic Era a new form of Megalithic tomb was constructed – the portal-grave or portal dolmen, a single-chambered tomb consisting of three or more upright stones supporting an enormous capstone, with two of them so placed that they look like a portal. The portal-grave builders seem to derive from the earlier court-grave civilization; however, the graves' main distribution is not in the court-grave region but largely in the east, not far from the coast. A capstone such as the massive granite boulder on the Browne's Hill dolmen in County Carlow might weigh up to 100 tons, and it was no mean feat of primitive engineering to raise one into position. Occasionally a portal-grave had two chambers and two capstones.

The dawn of the Metal Age

In the period shortly before 2000 BC there was considerable population movement in Europe in the east–west and south–north directions. Archaeological evidence in Ireland indicates that more than one immigrant group arrived at the end of the Neolithic Age, as the Metal Age dawned. The groups can be distinguished by the differences in their burial customs and funeral rituals as well as by the form and ornamentation of some of their artefacts. It is not clear, however, in what order these people reached Ireland or to what extent they intermingled; new traits and new artefacts appear but the early Neolithic tradition also persisted. The immigrants have been classified by the names of distinctive objects associated with their culture – Beaker People, Bowl Food Vessel People, Vase Food Vessel People, Urn People.

Browne's Hill dolmen, County Carlow. Long considered a pagan altar in popular fancy, the portal-grave or dolmen consists of a burial chamber formed by raising a large capstone on three or more 'portal' stones.

Vase-type food vessel found in a cist grave at Maganey Lower, County Kildare, with the cremated remains of an adult and child.

One characteristic of many of the newcomers was that they buried their dead singly, whether by inhumation or after cremation.

The Beaker People, who originated in eastern Europe, appear to have come into Ireland in two groups, some from Brittany into the south-west of Ireland and some from the Rhineland across Britain into the east of Ireland, where there was one prominent settlement in the Boyne valley. The Beaker People in the south-west favoured wedge-shaped tombs, of which between 400 and 500 are known, mostly in west Cork and Clare. On the Continent the Beaker People always buried their dead singly, but in Ireland they were influenced by indigenous customs and some Beaker burials have been found in communal Megalithic tombs.

The art and rituals of the Food Vessel People, who came into Ireland through northern Britain, derived from the more widespread Beaker culture; they were probably of the same racial origin, all belonging to the single-grave culture which flourished in south Russia, Bohemia, Saxo-Thuringia and Jutland, along with a related style in pottery decoration. In Ireland the Food Vessel People continued to use single graves, practising inhumation and cremation. The Bowl Food Vessel People imported the custom of burying the inhumed corpse in a crouched position, together with a pottery vessel.

Although practically all of their implements were of stone or flint, the Beaker People knew of metal and seem to have brought a small quantity with them; they did produce the valuable innovation of the flat bronze axe. It is not difficult, therefore, to picture these newcomers in their excitement over metal and their new awareness of its value. Their presence in copper-rich west Cork suggests that experienced prospectors had come with them from Brittany. The success of the metal-seekers in discovering mineral wealth in Ireland ushered in a new age for the country and its inhabitants – the Bronze Age – which began about 1800 BC and reached its zenith in Ireland over a period of 1,000 years.

The Early Bronze Age

Ireland has fairly extensive mineral deposits. At Avoca, County Wicklow, the deposit of copper ore is so vast that while 3 million tons have been processed there is still a known reserve of at least 22 million tons. West Cork was particularly rich in copper ores – in the nineteenth century its mines were the most productive in Europe, but they lost their importance and were abandoned after the discovery of copper in Rhodesia. The principal mines were at Ballycummisk near Skull, at Brown Head and Streak Head near Crookhaven, at Allihies near Dursey Head and on the slopes of Mount Gabriel, County Cork, where the mine shafts date from the Early Bronze Age. Copper and lead were found in the valley of the River Roughty in County Kerry, lead and silver at Clonmines, County Wexford, lead and zinc at Glendalough, County Wicklow, once Ireland's major source of metals, and in the Silvermines Mountains in County Tipperary. Undoubtedly Ireland still has undiscovered mineral deposits; in recent years excellent deposits of silver, lead and zinc have been discovered at Tynagh, County Galway, where the ores lie in karstic hollows in the carboniferous limestone.

The metal prospectors of the Bronze Age certainly discovered the copper ores in Mount Gabriel, where the passages to their mines were found intact under blanket bog when it was cut for fuel. Carbon-14 tests on charcoal from the mouth of such quarries have given a date around 1500 BC. In his book *The Irish Landscape* Professor Frank Mitchell well describes the methods of the prehistoric miners.

We can thus picture the early miners, after they had located a suitable outcrop of ore, first lighting a fire against it to expand the rock, and then throwing on water to shrink and shatter it. The stone mauls, some of which were grooved to give a better purchase for a wicker handle, were then used both to free the shattered rock and to pound the fragments still further, so that the ore-rich pieces could be collected for smelting. If the richness of the ore made it worth following back into the rock, gradually a tunnel developed, and the diameters of the tunnel or holes in the hillside suggest that elaborate staging was not used, as they are about the size that would be excavated by a man standing on the ground, and using a handled hammer. The miners could only go a limited distance into the hillside, because beyond a certain point ventilation would become difficult, and seepage of water from the tunnel walls would make it difficult to apply heat effectively to them.

The passages were low and narrow, only about 2 ft high and 3 ft wide; the miners crawled through them to reach the mine itself, which was usually not more than 5 ft high.

A group of metal-using immigrants, distinguishable by their custom of cremating their dead and placing the remains under an inverted pottery bowl or urn in a single grave, seems to have arrived in Ireland about 1700 BC, early in the new metal-using era called the Bronze Age. Earlier evidence of this culture in northern Britain leaves little doubt that it was from there, through south-west Scotland, that the Urn People reached Ireland. Skilled smiths, they knew how to make leather and work bone.

New metal tools and implements appeared, looped spear-heads, daggers, halberds, dirks, rapiers, bronze razors and depilatory tweezers, which at first were cast in stone moulds or in sand. The inhabitants of Ireland also became interested in personal adornment. Among ornaments discovered are bronze bracelets and beads, jet and amber beads for necklaces, and necklaces of tubular copper and of segmented faience beads made by moulding and fusing blue glass and grains of quartz.

Gold ornaments, for which prehistoric Ireland is justly famous, were manufactured either from alluvial gold panned mainly in Wicklow or from imported gold. One of the earliest decorations was the lunula, a flat, crescent-shaped neck ornament fashioned from a thin sheet of gold, and usually engraved or incised with geometric motifs. Similar ornaments of the early Metal Age have been found on the continent of Europe, but none as refined or as elaborate as the Irish gold lunulae, which can be considered the first native artistic achievement.

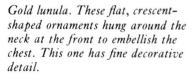

Gold lunula. These flat, crescent-shaped ornaments hung around the neck at the front to embellish the chest. This one has fine decorative detail.

Gold gorget from Gleninsheen, County Clare. Ireland is justly famous for its prehistoric gold objects; this one dates from 700 BC.

The Later Bronze Age

As the Bronze Age advanced and a greater supply of gold became available, talented goldsmiths advanced in both expertise and creative ideas to make the most beautiful gold artefacts of the era in Europe. As well as fine sheetwork they mastered the techniques of hammering, of hollow goldwork and gold plating, and they twisted very fine gold wire to achieve a delicate filigree effect. Fortunately a number of examples of their exquisite workmanship have survived – pins, dress-fasteners, penannular rings, brooches, bracelets, pendants, ear-rings, gorgets and torcs – often discovered by farm labourers while ploughing or cutting turf. Irish-made gold ornaments were exported in the Later Bronze Age for trading abroad.

There is particular evidence that a period of prosperity began about 1200 BC, when craftsmen like weavers, leather-workers, carpenters and bone-workers made progress. By the eighth century BC, when the bronze industry reached its zenith, the smiths were making great buckets and cauldrons and magnificent trumpets of sheet bronze; by that time clay moulds were used rather than stone ones. In recent years a bronze workshop of the Later Bronze Age was discovered in a hill-fort at Rathgall, County Wicklow.

The Celts

The arrival of the first Celts in Ireland cannot be dated from archaeological evidence. Known by the Greeks as *Keltoi*, large numbers of them dwelt in a homeland north of the Alps, stretching eastwards from the Rhine across what is now southern Germany and into Bohemia; however they never formed a unified ethnic group, but were divided into many tribes who vied for dominance. As the Celts were farmers, over-population in their homeland caused tension, so they expanded into new areas, westwards into France (Gaul), down to the Iberian peninsula, up to Britain and Ireland, eastwards into the Balkans and on as far as Asia Minor.

While some authorities claim a Celtic presence in Ireland as early as 1500 BC and others put the Celtic immigration as much as 1,000 years later, it seems reasonable to conclude that a substantial Celtic migration to Ireland occurred during the Hallstatt period of Celtic expansion in Europe. This began in the seventh century

BC, and coincides with a period beginning around 700 BC for which there is evidence of increased agricultural activity and increased prosperity in Ireland. Earlier stray Celts may have reached Ireland before that, and other settlers may have followed in the sixth century and again in the fourth century, when there was a further stream of Celtic expansion in Europe. By that time Greek writers ranked the *Keltoi* as the most numerous 'barbarian' peoples, along with the Scythians and Persians.

The earlier Metal Age settlers probably spoke an undifferentiated Indo-European language. The Celts brought with them a branch of Indo-European which developed into Goidelic, the name given to a group of Celtic languages originating in Ireland and distinguishable as a group from other Celtic tongues. Goidelic includes Irish (also called Gaelic or Erse), still spoken in Ireland, and its offshoots, Scottish Gaelic, still spoken in parts of Scotland, and Manx, formerly spoken in the Isle of Man.

Celtic scholars have discerned, not only in the shared linguistic roots but also in some cultural similarities, the ancient common heritage of the Celts and the people of India in a region west of the Urals and north of the Black Sea, where Indo-European speech originated. The similarity has been remarked, for example, between the Celtic ritual of horse sacrifice, practised in Ireland until the Middle Ages, and the Hindu *asvamehda*. Analogies can also be found between Hindu religious lore and what is known of the beliefs and practices of the Celts. The *Tuatha De* and the *Fomhoire*, the divine people and the demons of Irish Celtic mythology, can be compared with the Hindu *Devas* and *Asuras* who were similarly engaged in an interminable struggle. A prominent God in the Irish Celtic pantheon was Lugh, meaning 'The Shining One'; his epithet *Lamhfhada*, meaning 'of the long arm', is comparable to that of the Hindu God Savitar 'of the wide hand', although in his attributes Lugh was closer to the Hindu god-sovereign Varuna. The stratification of Irish Celtic society also has similarities with that of the distant Hindus – the druid or priest class, the warrior nobles and the freemen being comparable with the brahmins, the kshatriyas, and the vaishyas.

Goddesses also formed part of the Celtic pantheon; the most important in Ireland were the three daughters of Dahgda, the chief god of the Irish. All three were named Brigid, meaning 'the exalted one'; one was the patroness of poetry and learning, one of healing, and one of the smith's craft. Memory of these pagan goddesses is preserved in the mythology surrounding the life of their Christian namesake, St Brigid, whose widespread cult in Ireland appears to have followed that of her pagan predecessors. The goddess Anu, mother of the gods, is indirectly remembered in the name of twin hills in County Kerry once known as *Da Chich Anann* (The Paps of Anu) because of their breast-like contours, and still called 'The Paps'.

The Celts did not build places of worship; their ceremonies took place in open-air woodland sanctuaries rather than temples. Sacred trees, rivers and wells were objects of devotion; the tree cult was particularly persistent, each tribe in Ireland having its sacred tree. Although Christian Church leaders later denounced vows offered to trees and wells, these relics of the older faith lingered. By attaching new myths to pagan cult objects and cult sites, the Christian Church drew many of them into its orbit. Pagan superstitions about trees still exist: even today some country people will not cut down a thorn tree which has planted itself, but revere it as a 'fairy thorn', and rags and rosaries are still tied as offerings to trees near holy wells.

The pagan Celts in Ireland believed in the transmigration of souls and in an otherworld, sometimes thought of as subterranean, sometimes as islands beyond the western sea.

Hill-fort dwelling places

The hill-forts, of which about 50 are known in Ireland, can be dated to around 700 BC, so their appearance coincides with the probable arrival of the Celts. A large hilltop enclosure surrounded by an earthen bank and a ditch, the hill-fort seems to

have served as a fortification, a protected tribal residential compound, and also as a ritual centre. One important hill-fort, Navan Fort, near the present town of Armagh, covered an area of 18 acres. Other large hill-forts were at Rathgall, County Wicklow, Moghane, County Clare, where there were three concentric banks and ditches around the hilltop, and Dun Ailinne, County Kildare, where the area enclosed is no less than 40 acres. Some of the hill-forts, such as the one at Tara, County Meath, were certainly built on a site which previously had been used as a necropolis.

The Iron Age Iron-working, known in Armenia in the second millennium BC, seems to have spread into Europe after the collapse of the Hittite Empire, and became widespread in Europe during the second half of the eighth century BC. This knowledge was diffused in western and northern Europe by Celts of the Hallstatt culture, who eventually brought to Ireland the knowledge that iron was superior to bronze for many purposes and cheaper to produce.

Ring-fort dwelling places The sites of 30,000 or more ring-forts may be seen in Ireland. The ring-fort or rath was a dwelling place of the Iron Age consisting of a house or cluster of houses in a circular enclosure surrounded by an earthen bank and ditch. The name ring-fort implies a fortification, but it was really no more than a habitation with the minimum protection for the inhabitants and their livestock against marauders. Where stone

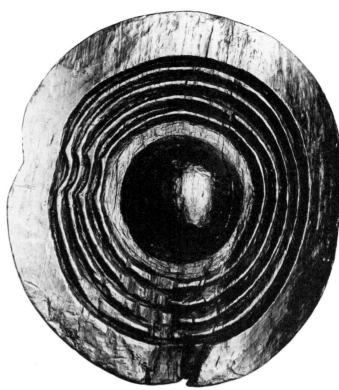

ABOVE *A Celtic warrior's shield made of alderwood, found in County Mayo.*

LEFT *Dun Aengus, Inishmore, Aran Islands. Perched high on the cliffs above the Atlantic, this magnificent stone fort has concentric defence walls and a jagged* chevaux-de-frise.

was plentiful the ring-forts were enclosed with a stone wall and those that were the seats of important chiefs, such as the great ring-fort in County Donegal, the Grianan of Ailech, were imposing edifices. The stone ring-fort Dun Aengus, perched on the cliffs of Inishmore in the Aran Islands, is one of the most magnificent and dramatic of its kind in Europe. Here there was certainly fortification – thousands of jagged stone stakes forming a *chevaux-de-frise* were placed close together outside the walls.

Another type of dwelling place dating from the Iron Age and, like some ring-forts, in continuing use until the late Middle Ages, was the crannog, an artificial island built up in a lake or marsh.

La Tène decoration

During the Iron Age artefacts were produced in Ireland in bronze and gold in the style called La Tène, which flourished among Celtic tribes on the Continent, originating between 450 and 400 BC; it is named after an archaeological site on Lake Neuchâtel in Switzerland. The La Tène decorative style, characterized by spirals, often tightly coiled, and swirling tendrils, had become established in Ireland by the third century BC. There are three good examples in Ireland of free-standing aniconic stones (which were probably used for ritual purposes), carved with spirals, trumpets and curvilinear swirls in the La Tène style. At Turoe, County Galway, there is a phallic stone monument brought from the Rath of Feerwore; there is another carved cult stone at Castlestrange, County Roscommon, and one in the National Museum of Ireland which was removed from Killycluggin, County Cavan. The sites of these

23

RIGHT *Two-faced head from Caldragh graveyard, Boa Island, County Fermanagh.*

OPPOSITE *The portrait of Christ from the Gospel of St Matthew in the* Book of Kells. *Jesus is shown with blonde hair and blue eyes, flanked by peacocks, symbols of the Resurrection.*

BELOW *Gold torc found at Broighter near Lough Foyle by a ploughman in 1896; it is decorated with swirling ornament in the La Tène style and closes with a sophisticated mechanism.*

RIGHT *Two-faced head from Caldragh graveyard, Boa Island, County Fermanagh.*

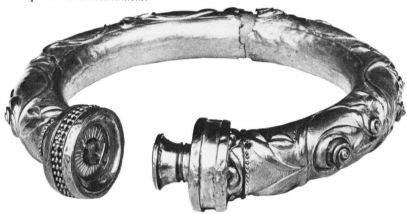

stones indicate how deeply the Celts and their culture had penetrated the heartland of Ireland by the last centuries BC. Among the more famous La Tène metal artefacts of the Iron Age are fragments of a bronze crown, now in the National Museum of Ireland and known as the Petrie crown, bronze discs and lids in the same museum, sword scabbards from Lisnacroghera, County Antrim, also made of bronze and now in the Ulster Museum, Belfast, and one of Ireland's great prehistoric treasures, a gold torc found by a ploughman at Broighter, County Derry, in 1896 and now in the National Museum of Ireland. This torc is remarkable not only for its exquisite workmanship but also for its sophisticated closing mechanism.

Pagan iconic monuments

FOLLOWING PAGES
LEFT *The Cross of Cong. Almost certainly made by a workman of Clonmacnoise early in the twelfth century, this processional cross, one of the last great artefacts of Early Christian art, shows Scandinavian influence.*

ABOVE RIGHT *Temple Benen, Inishmore, Aran Islands. A fine example of a single-chamber Early Christian church, superbly situated above Galway Bay.*

BELOW RIGHT *The Lismore crozier was made for an abbot of Lismore, County Waterford, between 1090 and 1113. It was found in 1814 walled up in a tower of Lismore Castle.*

Iconic stones found in Ireland and attributed to the Iron Age seem primitive in comparison with the aniconic sculpture. They usually represent a head, regarded by the Celts as the seat of the soul and therefore an important cult symbol. Examples of Janus heads, known in Continental pagan Celtic cult worship, have been found in Ireland, particularly in the upper Shannon region and the lakelands of Cavan and Fermanagh. The most impressive and mysterious is the great two-faced head in Caldragh graveyard on Boa Island in Lower Lough Erne, County Fermanagh. Three-faced heads have also been found, the most notable at Corleck, County Cavan. Cavan.

The eight carved figures found on White Island in Lower Lough Erne were once thought to have been pagan idols, but these unusual effigies belong to the period after the conversion of the population to Christianity.

2 Celtic Christian Ireland

By the fifth century AD, which offers the earliest evidence of Christian activity in Ireland, the Celts had been established there for a thousand years. Though the traditions and beliefs of the earlier inhabitants remained, the settlement of the sophisticated Celts had had an enormous impact on a people on whom they had imposed their language, customs, culture and social structure. After a millennium the insular Celtic civilization, which had developed and flourished, was firmly entrenched in Ireland, while elsewhere in Europe the Celtic way of life had been disrupted by the expansion of the Roman Empire, by the introduction of Christianity, and by the Germanic invasions.

An alphabetic script, called Ogham after Ogmios (or Ogma), the pagan Celtic god of eloquence, was perfected in Ireland in the fourth century AD. In its simplest form this alphabet consisted of twenty letters which were depicted by four sets of from one to five incised notches, one set obliquely across a dividing line, one set vertically across the line, one set to the left and another to the right of the line. Usually the corner of a stone was used as the dividing line. A fifth set of five extra letters was a later development. Most of the surviving inscriptions in Ogham are on memorial stones, and give the name and patronymic of a person. Several hundred vertical incised stones have been found in Ireland, principally in the south-west, and about 40 in south Wales, 10 in the Isle of Man and a few in Cornwall, all areas of Irish influence through migration from Ireland to western Britain in the fourth century.

As a result of advances in agriculture the diet became more varied. Wheat, barley, rye, oats, peas and beans are mentioned in Irish Celtic tracts. Milk was drunk in various forms, as well as being churned into butter or eaten as curds. Meat was boiled by being plunged into a trough of water which had been heated by the immersion of very hot stones. This method of cooking, dating from the Bronze Age, was widely used in the Iron Age and continued until the Middle Ages. There is evidence that some goods were imported, but trade was desultory and the inhabitants of Ireland were largely self-sufficient. By the fifth century the coulter-plough was in use in Ireland; with a vertical iron knife attached to its frame this plough could cut through matted roots as it was drawn along, and aided the clearing of ground for agriculture. Irish smiths also manufactured a fairly wide range of tools and farming implements – axes, adzes, hammers, chisels, awls, bill hooks, gouges and saws. An important community occupying a large rath had its own resident craftsmen, but the population was largely served by itinerant craftsmen who travelled the country from rath to rath. The smiths, the most important of these mobile artisans, would set up a forge on arriving at a rath, manufacture the objects required and then move on to another community. Some social historians see in those itinerant smiths the distant origins of the Irish travelling people of today, long known as tinkers because, until

OPPOSITE *Dunbrody Abbey, County Wexford, founded in the early 1180s. Most of the ruins to be seen today are from the thirteenth century.*

recent years, mending metal utensils as they travelled about the country was their principal means of livelihood.

The country was divided into about 150 little kingdoms, called *tuatha*, each with its own monarch. Groups of *tuatha* united in acknowledging the rule of a greater king over their individual kingdoms. Eventually a high king emerged who attempted to establish his sovereignty of the whole island over the other monarchs, but it was not until well into the Christian period that the high kingship became effective.

Within each *tuath* the society was divided into four principal classes united by relationships of mutual obligation. At the top was the monarch of the *tuath* with his family group, which extended over four generations to include the descendants of a common great-grandfather. All the males in the rulers' family group were eligible to succeed to the kingship on his death. The choice of the successor frequently led to a bitter struggle between the candidates, who often resorted to murder or to maiming, since a man with a physical deformity was excluded from kingship. The second class comprised the rest of the nobles, mostly warriors, but it also included the druids, the bards (on whose oral records the society relied for its knowledge of the laws), and some craftsmen. Freemen, mostly farmers, comprised the third class and bondsmen or slaves the fourth.

St Patrick

It was as a slave that Patrick, the national apostle of the Irish, first came to Ireland. The Irish habitually raided the coasts of western Britain and Scotland, and brought back large numbers of captives as slaves. Irish raiders snatched Patrick from his home in Roman Britain when he was sixteen and brought him to Ireland where he spent six miserable years before managing to escape. Patrick was born a Christian, the son of a deacon and the grandson of a priest. Some time after his return home, as he recounts in his spiritual autobiography the *Confessio*, he experienced a vivid dream in which he heard the voices of the Irish calling him back. Accepting this call, Patrick eventually returned and devoted his life to preaching the divinity of Christ to the heathen Irish.

In 431 Pope Celestine sent a prelate named Palladius from Gaul to be the first Christian bishop in Ireland. Palladius probably knew St Germanus, who had helped to effect the consolidation of the Church in Britain by suppressing heresy there. Germanus was Bishop of Auxerre from 418 until his death in 448. According to Patrick's seventh-century biographer Muirchú, Patrick spent some years in Auxerre, but this assertion has been doubted because of Patrick's imperfect Latin. However, Muirchú has it that Patrick was consecrated by a bishop named Amathorex; the name may well be a corruption of the name of Germanus's immediate predecessor as Bishop of Auxerre, St Amator, who died in 418. Possibly Patrick was in Gaul before 418 but not for long enough to perfect his Latin. If so, his mission in Ireland may have commenced in the 420s, and it could therefore have been to his converts that Palladius was sent. On the other hand, it is generally accepted that there must have been some Christians in Ireland before Patrick's mission began – slaves and converts from haphazard contacts with Christians in Britain, Scotland or Gaul. The Irish annals (which are often inaccurate on fifth-century dates) give 432 as the beginning of Patrick's mission, and this is the traditionally accepted date. It is curiously close to the date of Palladius's appointment, and there is evidence that the two may have been confused by early chroniclers. Exact evidence on which to pin the dates of Patrick's life and missionary activities is lacking. Mention of the Franks as heathens in Patrick's *Epistola* at least proves that he wrote it before the mass conversion of the Franks in 496, and indicates that he was probably writing when the Franks were invading Gaul from 428 onwards. Another school of historians puts Patrick's arrival as a missionary in the 450s/460s.

It is most probable, then, that Patrick's mission in Ireland took place in the second or third quarter of the fifth century. This mission was an outstanding success owing to his zeal, his exceptional moral and spiritual stature and his sensitivity, which enabled him to understand and respect a heroic society. He restricted himself to his aim, which was to persuade the Irish to accept Christ and to abandon idolatry, and did not attempt to change the existing social structure or interfere with its taboos, its honour codes or its particular legal system. Indeed he deferred to those local customs in which he saw nothing objectionable to the Christian faith. He went about, for example, with a retinue of young nobles and distributed gifts to the kings. Such conduct was criticized by the hierarchy abroad, who were dismayed by this unorthodox behaviour and accused Patrick of simony.

It is doubtful whether all the Irish were converted in Patrick's lifetime – there were probably still heathens in Ireland in the sixth century. In any case pagan beliefs and superstitions lingered on for centuries; sometimes even the clergy reverted to pagan practices, such as magic rites and the preparing of potions. However, Patrick left behind him a well-organized Christian community with an episcopal administration.

The first Christian churches

The first places of Christian worship in Patrick's time were similar to the simple domestic dwellings of a rath. As population groups were small there was no call for large churches. The Christians assembled and worshipped in huts built of mud or timber, or sometimes of timber and wattle. The early mud chapels have long since vanished but traces of early timber churches have been found by archaeologists, for example at Ardagh, County Longford, where St Mel is said to have founded a church in the fifth century, and at Church Island near Valentia, County Kerry, where the foundations of a wooden church measuring only 6×9 ft were found beneath the remains of a larger early stone church.

The timber churches were built by skilled craftsmen. The seventh-century *Book of Mulling* praises St Gobban, described as a master craftsman in both wood and stone, who built a church for St Mullin and roofed it with shingles of yew wood from a sacred pagan tree, the *eo rossa*. The Irish tradition of church-building in wood is affirmed by the Venerable Bede, who wrote early in the eighth century of the church at Lindisfarne that it was built 'not of stone, but in the Irish manner, of hewn oak and covered with reeds'. This tradition of building churches in wood continued in Ireland long after the twelfth century, when St Bernard of Clairvaux described a church at Bangor, County Down, as 'made of strong planks closely and strongly fastened together, an Irish work not devoid of beauty'.

While most of the early Christian wooden churches were small, modest buildings, there is at least one exception – St Brigid's church at Kildare – and surely Armagh and other important ecclesiastical centres would have had edifices to equal it. A description of the wooden church at Kildare, written about 630, tells us that it rose to 'a dizzy height'; inside, the panels were painted with frescoes and there were linen hangings on the east wall. This church was burned in the eighth century and nothing survives of the richly embellished sarcophagi of St Conleath and St Brigid, encased in gold and silver and encrusted with gems and precious stones, or even of the gold and silver crowns which hung over them.

The introduction of Christianity created a need for chalices, altar vessels, reliquaries, bells and book covers. This provided a challenge and a stimulus for the talented Irish craftsmen whose workshops included facilities for making *millefiori*, which entailed fusing together glass rods of different colours. One *millefiori* manufactory at Lagore, County Meath, also made glass bracelets and glass studs for ornamental inlays. The metalworkers could produce exquisite filigree work, enamelwork and chip carving. These arts reached their zenith in the eighth century.

Monasticism   By the eighth century the monastic system dominated the life of the Church in Ireland. Monasticism of the kind associated with the coenobitic communities of the Desert Fathers in the Near East and eastern Europe was adopted in Ireland by the end of the fifth century, before St Bernard had established his monastery and rule at Monte Cassino. So great was the appeal of monastic life in Ireland and so rapidly did it spread there that, within a century of Patrick's mission, his episcopal organization was being replaced by one in which abbots supplanted bishops as the effective leaders of the Church. This changeover was facilitated by the rural and tribal nature of Irish society. The usual pattern in the Church elsewhere was for the seat of a bishop to be a town of some importance from which the diocese was ruled. In Ireland there were no such towns. As the larger monasteries flourished it was they that became the most important centres in the country.

It can be claimed that the cradle of Irish monasticism was the monastery of Candida Casa at Whithorn in western Scotland (called Rosnat by the Irish) which was founded early in the fifth century by St Ninian, the first Christian missionary to Scotland. St Enda, a native of Ulster who died about 530, was trained at Candida Casa. Returning to Ireland, he founded his own community in the isolation of the storm-lashed Aran Islands on Inishmore; this remote monastery became a celebrated novitiate and spiritual centre. Another fifth-century alumnus of Candida Casa, St Mochaoi, chose a pre-Christian settlement at Nendrum on Strangford Lough, County Down, for the site of his monastic foundation. Three concentric dry-stone cashels survive; a church, a school, and at least four dwelling huts stood within the innermost enclosure, and a pottery and a smithy functioned between this enclosure and the middle one. St Finnian of Moville was trained in this monastery at Nendrum and at Candida Casa.

Each monastery followed the rule established by its own founder, whose successors to the abbacy were frequently the founder's kin and not necessarily ordained priests or deacons. The monastic communities ranged in size from little establishments, with as few as a dozen monks or nuns, to large and powerful foundations like Clonard in County Meath, with its famous school founded by the elder St Finnian who died in 549. Finnian was surrounded by disciples, among whom were those known as the Twelve Apostles of Ireland, who eventually created their own monastic foundations. One of these was St Brendan the Navigator, who is reputed to have crossed the Atlantic in a curragh-type boat, a feat which has recently been proved possible. St Brendan founded the monastery at Clonfert, County Galway, in about 560. St Ciaran, born about 516, was another of the twelve; he, with eight companions, founded the great monastery at Clonmacnoise, to which students thronged from all over Ireland. St Comgall, an Irish Pict, another of the twelve, founded a monastery of exceptional importance in about 558 at Bangor, County Down. The best known of the Clonard Twelve must be St Columba, also called Columcille, who was born of a princely family in north-eastern Donegal in 521, and studied first at the monastery of Moville, near his home, under its founder the younger St Finnian, himself an alumnus of Candida Casa. Columcille founded a monastery on the Scottish isle of Iona and a chain of important monasteries in Ireland, at Derry, at Durrow in County Offaly, at Kells in County Meath, and possibly others.

The peregrini   Irish monasteries became centres of learning, whose influence was not restricted to Ireland; a stream of educated missionary monks went out from them to spread their faith and culture in foreign lands. Expecting nothing, these dedicated men were willing to endure hardships in order to impart their knowledge. The most prominent of these *peregrini* was the St Columba better remembered as Columban or Columbanus, who was born in Leinster about 540. After early studies in grammar, rhetoric, geometry and the Bible, Columban went to a monastery at Gleenish on Lough Erne,

County Fermanagh, and then to Bangor where he remained for about twenty-five years under the founder-abbot, St Comgall, until he left for the Continent. With his companions, Columban first founded monasteries in eastern France – at Anne-gray and then at Luxeuil, where hundreds flocked to join the community; these were followed by one at Bobbio in northern Italy. One of Columban's companions, Deicola, founded the monastery at Lure in France, and another, St Gall, whose name is perpetuated in the Swiss city of St Gallen, converted the Alemanni tribe to Christianity. By the end of the seventh century, within a hundred years of Columban's missionary activity, there were about sixty monasteries following his severe, ascetic rule in the territories of the Franks. Another Irish missionary *peregrinus*, St Fursa, founded a monastery in eastern Britain at Burghcastle and others in Gaul, one of which, at Péronne on the River Somme, became a noted Irish monastic centre. Fursa's brother, St Foillan, founded a monastery at Fosses in what is now Belgium. St Killian, who left Ireland with twelve companions at 643, settled at Würzburg in Germany, and was murdered there in 689 at the instigation of the Duchess of Thuringia; she was irate because Killian had rebuked her husband for marrying her, his brother's widow. Many hospices too were founded and run by the Irish, such as the one founded by St Fiacra in the seventh century beside his monastery at Meaux.

Irish scholarship flourished abroad in the eighth and ninth centuries. Feargal or Vergil, the Irish Abbot-Bishop of Salzburg, was probably the author of the curious *Cosmographia*. Irish scholars, many of whom were monks who no longer favoured the ascetic life, were at the court and schools of the Emperor Charlemagne. One, Dungal, who left Ireland in about 784, attempted in a letter to the Emperor in 811 to explain the eclipse of the sun in the previous year. The first medieval treatise on geography, the *Liber de mensura orbis terrae*, was the work of another Irish expatriate, Dicuil, in 825. A company of Irish scholars arrived at the court of Charles the Bald at Liège in 848. This king, crowned Emperor in 875, gave particular protection at Liège to the Irish literary celebrity Sedulius Scottus, a versatile metrical poet, scriptural scholar, commentator and author. His work *On Christian Rulers* was written to guide Charles the Bald, and the Empress Irmingard reproduced some of his Latin verses in needlework. Donatus, the Irish Bishop of Fiesole, near Florence, who established a nunnery of St Brigid at Piacenza in northern Italy in the ninth century, was also an accomplished poet.

So numerous were the Irish in France in the latter half of the ninth century that Heiric of Auxerre was prompted to write in 870, 'Almost all Ireland, disregarding the sea, is migrating to our shores with a flock of philosophers.' The most illustrious of these expatriates was the brilliant and pious philosopher-theologian known as John Scotus Eriugena. He was the author of a profound and daringly original work, written in dialogue form in about 867 and entitled *De Divisione Naturae* (*On The Division of Nature*). Eriugena's pre-eminent mastery of Greek enabled him to translate the *Pseudo Dionysius*, which notably affected Western thought, veering away from the Western tradition towards the Neo-Platonic approach in his philosophy, which incorporates and transforms theology.

The principal areas of influence of the Irish men of learning were Northumbria and the Frankish Empire. But they travelled south as far as Italy, and also eastwards; a small Irish-type church has been excavated in Czechoslovakia in the heart of Moravia. Eventually, from the Irish monastery at Regensburg in Bavaria, Irish monks reached Kiev in Russia in the eleventh century, where they were received and given valuable gifts by the ruling prince.

The Irish monasteries

In the monasteries in Ireland, where the erudite expatriates received their training and education, a high standard of learning and artistic achievement was maintained.

Eloquence, prized by the pagan Celts who had relied on oral instruction, was still esteemed by the Christian Celts. Intellectual discussion in the monastic schools stimulated thought. In one of his sharp written exchanges with Pope Boniface IV, St Columban reminded the pontiff of 'the freedom of discussion characteristic of my native land'.

There is an inclination to think of Irish monasteries primarily in terms of little isolated communities like the one on Skellig Michael Island off the coast of Kerry; a place where the monks sought a life far from worldly care and temptation, it consists only of six beehive-hut dwellings and two chapels. However, there were large monasteries too, such as Bangor which at one time claimed a community of 4,000, or Clonmacnoise with 3,000. Such monasteries assumed the proportions of a village. The standard of discipline and austerity varied from one monastery to another, but they all aimed to be self-supporting, engaging in agriculture, horticulture, pisciculture, bee-keeping and animal husbandry. In these they were aided by the *manaig*, who seem to have been lay brethren living on the monastic estate under a contractual agreement with the abbot rather than under his rule of religious obedience.

Clochan na Carraige, Kilmurvy, Inishmore, Aran Islands. A large stone beehive hut.

The scribes Writing was considered an art rather than a mere utility. Any monastery of consequence had its scriptorium, where monks who were fine calligraphers and illuminators worked with goose or swan quills on vellum, copying manuscripts which were made into codices. They strove to create a thing of beauty of each text. The psalter known as the *Cathach of Columba* has traditionally been attributed to the hand of St Columcille himself. Whether or not this is so it appears to have been written at the end of the sixth century, either in his lifetime or shortly after his death. Because it pre-dates the first Irish mission to Northumbria in 634 it is unaffected by Anglo-Saxon influence. About one half of the original work survives – fifty-eight pages, 9 × 6 ins – written in a fine majuscule script; the decorative motifs – trumpet patterns and spirals, for example – derive from La Tène art.

After Irish scribes had visited Northumbria, an art usually described as 'Insular' developed, in which Anglo-Saxon influence is discernible. The *Book of Durrow*, which dates from the second half of the seventh century, is an early masterpiece of this school. It is a Vulgate text of the four Gospels in majuscule script on pages very slightly larger than those of the *Cathach*. Although the scribe used the Vulgate text, the arrangement of the Gospels and the symbols of the four evangelists are in

the Old Latin version with which the Irish monks were more familiar. The elaborate decoration in red, green, yellow and brown on a black background is often exquisite in its detail. The Celtic origin of most of the ornament is obvious but Anglo-Saxon influence is evident, for example, in the interlaced animal decoration. Coptic and Syriac manuscripts must also have been available to the Irish monks, for there are striking similarities in both colour and layout between the *Book of Durrow* and Coptic manuscripts from the Near East.

In time, to economize on the use of vellum, Irish scribes adopted a reduced majuscule script, sometimes described as half-uncial. This was the script used by the three scribes who worked on the famous manuscript Gospels, once described as 'the great Gospel of Columkille, the chief relic of the Western World', and now known as the *Book of Kells*. Originally this splendid work consisted of about 370 pages measuring about $14\frac{1}{2} \times 10$ ins; 340 pages, trimmed to $13 \times 9\frac{1}{2}$ ins, survive. The *Book of Kells* dates from the last decade of the eighth century or the first decades of the ninth. It may have been planned in honour of St Columcille on the bicentenary of his death in 797, and its first scribe was possibly Connachtach, described in the annals as an 'Eminent scribe and Abbot of Iona' at his death in 802. This was also the year of the first Viking attack on Iona, and it looks as though the partly finished precious work was then taken to Kells for safety, to be completed by scribes and painters there. The iconographical background of the *Book of Kells* is complex, and connection with other sources is elusive; it appears that the images were inspired by the local spirit of the age. Most of the decorative motifs belong to the Insular repertoire, with the exception of foliage patterns similar to those in some Anglo-Saxon manuscripts believed to have been penned and decorated at Lindisfarne. The *Book of Kells* also departs from the Insular tradition in its continuous decoration and the extensive use of full-page illustrations. The first of these shows the Virgin and Child, the earliest representation of them in a western manuscript, surrounded by golden-haired, winged angels carrying flabella. The Virgin is depicted with long fair tresses, wearing a brownish-purple mantle and stiffly enthroned. Her head and torso face forwards but her throne, with animal terminals, and her legs are shown sideways. The Child on her lap, in a green robe, is shown in profile, holding her hand. There can be little doubt that originally there was a full-page illustration of each of the evangelists, but only the portraits of Matthew and John have survived. They are shown full-face, seated; both have elegantly patterned robes. To many people, however, the real glory of the *Book of Kells* lies in the amazing wealth of intricate ornamental detail, in the strange, Egyptian-looking birds and beasts and the grotesque figures, so inventively contorted to form initial letters.

Approximately contemporary with the *Book of Kells* is the *Book of Armagh*, dictated to the scribe Ferdomnach in the monastery of Armagh by Abbot Torbach, who died in 808. It contains the four Gospels, with the Vulgate symbols for the evangelists – the angel, the lion, the bull and the eagle; it also includes the *Liber Angeli*, a text compiled from different sources, outlining Armagh's claims to property, to legal and ecclesiastical jurisdiction, and to privileges.

As well as martyrologies and litanies which display poetic talent and scholarship, Irish monastic literature is also rich in hagiography. The earliest formal hagiography is the *Life of Brigid* by Cogitosus, written about 650, which contains a description of the splendid wooden church at Kildare. This work abounds in accounts of miraculous occurrences with origins in folklore. Muirchú, the son or spiritual son of Cogitosus, was the author of a later seventh-century work, the *Life of Patrick*, a copy of which is the first item in the *Book of Armagh*. Another famous Irish hagiography is the *Life of Columcille*, a learned, historically accurate work written at the end of the seventh century by Adamnán, Abbot of Iona, and surviving in a manuscript written before 713.

The scribes also recorded the body of ecclesiastical legislation, the Canons which were the deliberations of the early synods, the Penitentials which prescribed the correct penance for transgressions, and the Cána. Apart from one, which regulated sabbath observance, the Cána were laws attributed to particular saints.

The ninth-century *Navigatio Brendani*, which relates the supposed voyage and adventures of St Brendan and his companions, is a fascinating combination of classical tradition, Christian legend, fairy tale and imaginative writing forming a narrative full of enchantment and excitement.

Secular writing and poetry

Secular books, too, were written and copied in the monastic scriptoria. Grammar was considered very important in the monastic schools, so the teachers compiled treatises on Latin grammar for their students. One of these early Irish Latin grammarians was Malsachan whose seventh-century work, glossed about 700, survives in two ninth-century manuscripts. There is a seventh-century manuscript in Irish minuscule script of the text of St Isidore of Seville's *Etymologiae*, an encyclopedia of human and divine subjects in which the liberal arts are applied to subjects such as anthropology, cosmology and history. The *Etymologiae*, which remained a primary work of reference for centuries, and was one of the most studied books of the Dark Ages and the Middle Ages, is also a landmark in glossography. The text, by an Irish scribe, indicates that the writings of this great Doctor of the Church, who died in 636 in Seville, reached the Irish world at an early date.

A class of learned laymen, the *Filid*, continued from pre-Christian times. They were poets, experts in secular law, historians and genealogists whose learning belonged to the old tradition, in which information was memorized and spread by word of mouth. From the mid-seventh century there is evidence that monastic scribes were recording the law tracts, genealogies, pagan mythologies and mythopoetic heroic sagas which passed as history. The sagas may have some historical content but they are not history as it is commonly accepted for they spring from a tradition in which exaggeration was an accepted convention, and were addressed to a public which demanded entertainment rather than facts. The *Táin Bó Cualnge* (*The Cattle Raid of Cooley*), the longest tale in the Ulster Cycle, in which Cú Chulainn is the hero, appears to have been formulated in the fourth century just before the coming of Christianity, and to have been first recorded in the mid-seventh century; but its beginning may be even earlier, in the Iron Age about whose customs it is informative; the earliest surviving texts are two ninth-century versions.

If it seems odd to us that Christian monks should painstakingly record a hotch-potch of pagan mythology and imaginative 'history', it surely seems even stranger that they carefully penned the lusty account in the *Leabhar Gabhála* (*The Book of Invasions*), of an orgy in which the two first men in Ireland died from their sexual exertions with 51 women and the third man fled for his life, 'lest he, too, by love be rent'. From this and other texts it is clear that the scribes were not prudes.

The nature poems composed by the Irish monks also reveal that these ascetic men did not lack a sensitive, and even sensual, appreciation of nature. The poems, full of delight in life, are usually concise and imaginative, with a complicated system of rhyming and alliteration which is lost in translation from the Old Irish.

There was no discrimination against women in the literary world of Celtic Christian Ireland, which produced a succession of talented women poets. In the ninth century Liadan of Corcaguiney, County Kerry, the first of these women poets of whom records exist, was a fully fledged member of the guild of poets, an achievement which entailed many years of study. In a poignant lament she expressed her feelings over rejecting her suitor, the poet Cuirithir, because of her religious convictions and despite her passionate love for him.

The Ardagh Chalice, named for the place where it was found in 1868 in County Limerick, was made in the eighth century of silver with gold and enamel decoration.

The annals

In a number of monasteries monks were engaged in compiling chronicles of important events, day by day. In the eighth century contemporary chronicles were probably kept at Iona, Clonmacnoise and Lismore, as well as in other monasteries. The surviving annals are all much later compilations, the work of scribes who apparently had access to early chronicles since lost, and also, it would appear, to a chronicle which was an amalgamated compilation of the eighth century, also lost. The earliest text to survive is a transcript of the *Annals of Innisfallen*, which begins with a section copied in 1092. A fragment of the *Annals of Tigernach* dates from the twelfth century; the Abbot Tigernach of Clonmacnoise himself died in 1088. The *Annals of Ulster*, the most complete series, was only in the course of compilation much later, in the fifteenth century, while the *Annals of the Four Masters* was not compiled until the seventeenth.

Metal artefacts

The resourceful creativity of the scribes and the themes and patterns of the manuscripts are mirrored in the fine metalwork and some of the stone sculpture of the Celtic Christian era. The virtuosity of the *Book of Kells* might be compared in metalwork to the perfection of the Ardagh Chalice, so named because it was found in 1868 in a field at Ardagh, County Limerick, by a lad digging potatoes. This priceless chalice is exquisitely fashioned in silver, gold and brass, and decorated with a rock crystal boss and studs of coloured enamel and glass. Even the base of the chalice, which would have been seen only by the priest when he raised it at the elevation, is finely decorated. A more recent find of Celtic Christian treasure is a bronze receptacle fashioned to look like a belt, and seemingly made to contain a saint's belt. This reliquary, known as the Moylough Belt Shrine, was found in a bog in County Sligo in 1945. It has *millefiori* as well as enamel and silver decoration.

Ample work and scope for skilled artisans was provided by the needs of the monasteries – for bells, altar vessels, reliquaries, book-shrines and crucifixion plaques – and of the laity, whose most popular item of jewellery was the penannular brooch; this served a practical as well as a decorative purpose as it was used to fasten cloaks. The most precious brooch found so far, surely once the personal property of a monarch, was found on the beach at Bettystown, County Meath. Known as the Tara Brooch, this masterpiece must have been made, like the Ardagh Chalice, about the time that the scribes were at work on the *Book of Kells*. It is made of bronze, covered at the front with gold foil and at the back with silvered copper, and set with studs of glass and amber. The filigree designs, panels of interlace and bosses all recall the workmanship of the Ardagh Chalice so precisely that some art historians have speculated that they are the work of the same master, or at least from the same workshop. Other, less costly, brooches such as the Cavan Brooch, while less impressive, are objects of considerable refinement and beauty, witness to the technical aptitude and disciplined artistic genius of the craftsmen of the Celtic Christian golden age.

Sculpture

A stone pillar, which can be dated from its inscription, stands about a quarter of a mile from the present border between Northern Ireland and the Irish Republic, at Kilnasaggart, County Armagh; the inscription records the dedication of its site by one Ternohc, son of Ceran. The death of this Ternohc is recorded in the annals in 714–16. On one side the pillar is carved with 10 encircled crosses, on the other is the inscription and a second, free-standing, cross within a circle. The stone carvers progressed in time to more elaborate memorial slabs and monuments, such as the eighth-century cross at Carndonagh, County Donegal, carved on one side with a cross formed of interlacing and with figures which appear to represent Christ, with outstretched hands, and the four evangelists.

The climax of the sculptor's art in the Celtic Christian period came with the high cross – a free-standing, self-contained monument comprising various sections and frequently ringed at the junction of the shaft and arms. Unlike the incised pillars and slabs which were usually funerary monuments, the high crosses were intended to be didactic and/or to inspire prayer and meditation. Most of the Irish high crosses date from the eighth to the tenth centuries and many originally stood in the precincts of monasteries. For some reason the taste for these monuments did not extend to the south-west. No high crosses have been found in Cork, Kerry or Limerick, although all three counties have other Celtic Christian remains, nor in Mayo or the western part of County Galway.

A group of crosses within a few miles of Carrick-on-Suir, which may be the work of the same mason or school, have a close analogy to eighth-century metalwork. Of these, the most striking are two high crosses in a graveyard at Ahenny, County Tipperary. Two others in the group, both elaborately carved, can be seen in County Kilkenny, one at Kilkieran, where there are two plain crosses in addition, and the other at Killamery. The Ahenny high crosses are so completely covered with sharply cut interlacings and spirals that they at once recall the *horror vacui* of the scribes, who desired to fill all the available space with decoration, while the bosses in high relief on the upright and the widely spread arms of the cross recall the stud decoration of contemporary metalwork.

The granite high cross at Moone, County Kildare, is almost half as high again as the Ahenny crosses, measuring about 17 ft. Its base is carved with scenes from the Old and New Testaments with flat, stylized figures reduced to geometrical shapes. On one side the Twelve Apostles are naively depicted as 12 identical, armless, square-bodied, gnome-like figures with out-turned feet. Other scenes portray a figure similar to Daniel in the lion's den, with three open-mouthed lions on each side; two fishes and five circular loaves depict the miracle of the multiplication of the loaves and

This silver brooch, found in County Tipperary, is ornamented with gold filigree and amber studs on the pinhead and terminal; it is a superior example of a kind widely manufactured in the eighth to the tenth centuries.

fishes; a less geometrical Adam and Eve face each other across a snake-entwined tree trunk. Other scenes, with a variety of animals and figures, are enigmatic. Figures on high crosses at Kells, County Meath, are more realistic in their depiction of biblical scenes. This work, close in style to a high cross at Iona, may date from the ninth century, when Kells grew in importance after Vikings attacked St Columba's Scottish island monastery.

At Monasterboice, County Louth, can be seen the work of a more talented sculptor; his figures, carved in high relief, have an easy, graceful plasticity and he had a remarkable sense of composition, placing several figures in a panel without over-crowding. The Cross of Muiredach at Monasterboice may have been erected by the Abbot Muiredach who died in 844, or by the later and more prominent abbot of the same name, a Muiredach who died in 922 or 923; its similarity to the Cross of the Scriptures at Clonmacnoise, erected around 910, points to the later date for Muire-dach's cross and for another beautiful high cross of the same school at Durrow, County Offaly.

A tenth-century gaming board for a peg-game found on a crannog in County Westmeath gives an idea of the skill of the wood carver.

Before leaving the sculptors we might remember those strange effigies on White Island in County Fermanagh which were mentioned earlier in connection with the pagan idols. They were built into the wall of a late twelfth-century church, presumably because they were considered unsuitable for the new place of worship. These effigies are unique in that no other Celtic Christian figure sculpture has been found in Ireland.

The early churches of which remains survive are all small, stark buildings. Even

LEFT *The door of St Fechin's, Fore, County Westmeath, showing the typical arrangement with flat head and inclined jambs that was usual in the single-chamber stone churches.*

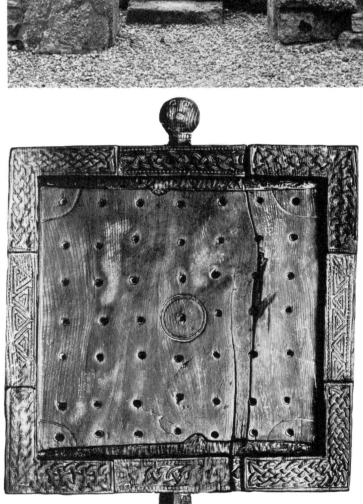

ABOVE LEFT *Tenth-century yew wood gaming board found in a crannog at Ballinderry, County Westmeath.*

ABOVE *One of the strange effigies on White Island, County Fermanagh, which were built into the wall of the late twelfth-century church, presumably because they were considered unsuitable for the new place of worship.*

after stone churches had become popular by the tenth and eleventh centuries they were still on a small scale and utterly simple.

The single-chamber stone churches

The first mention of a stone-built church occurs in the annals in 789 when a man was murdered at the doorway of a stone church at Armagh. From the remains of the 30–40 early stone churches still standing in various parts of Ireland we know that they were small single-chamber buildings. The earliest were built of immense stones, sometimes measuring as much as $5 \times 2 \times 3$ ft and without mortar; 20–30×15–20 ft was the usual size range of these little rectangular churches, which were frequently covered by a steeply pitched stone roof in the style of the earlier timber buildings. A simple, flat-headed doorway with inclined jambs was the usual entrance at the west end, and normally only a narrow loop-type window in the east wall lit the interior. Often the south and north walls projected to form antae.

In western Kerry there are the remains of little stone churches built in the form of an inverted boat; the best example is at Gallarus on the Dingle Peninsula, measuring externally 23×16 ft but with 4 ft thick walls.

The round towers

Tall, slender, skilfully constructed stone towers with conical roofs, now known as round towers, were called in Irish *cloigtheach*, meaning bell-house. This indicates that their principal purpose was as a steeple from which a bell could be tolled to call the monks in from the fields to their office. As the towers were mostly built with the door well above ground and without an external stone stair for comfortable access, they seem also to have served as a safe place for the monks and their valuables in time of attack; the monks could climb in, withdraw the ladder, close the door and watch attackers from the security of an upper window. A watchman on the top floor also had an excellent look-out post and could ring the bell to warn the community if he saw approaching enemies. The earliest round towers date from the end of the ninth or beginning of the tenth century, the latest from the twelfth.

There are examples at various early ecclesiastical sites, such as at Clonmacnoise and on the Rock of Cashel, at Drumlane, County Cavan, at Dysert O'Dea, County Clare, on Devenish Island, County Fermanagh, at the edge of Antrim town, at Cloyne, County Cork, and at Ardmore, County Waterford. At Kinneigh, County Cork, the lower part of the tower is hexagonal, at Clondalkin, County Dublin the tower has an external stair and still has its original conical roof, as does the round tower at Lusk in the same county. At Grangefertagh, County Kilkenny, the 100-ft high tower has eight storeys. The wide distribution of these towers bears witness to the presence of skilful builders in the country by the tenth and eleventh centuries.

The Vikings

The first recorded Viking raid on Irish soil was in 795, and sporadic incursions continued throughout the ninth and tenth centuries. Because of their treasuries, the monasteries bore the brunt of these violent attacks in which the raiders carried off what spoils they could, and because the annals which record these raids were compiled in the monasteries, an exaggerated view may be given of the damage and disruption. Largely because of this and due to the lack of contrary evidence, it was the general opinion in the past that the Vikings – cruel, ruthless barbarians – came to the saintly, civilized land of Ireland and violently broke up its advanced culture. In recent years historians and archaeologists have revised this viewpoint and, while admitting to a disruptive element in the Viking presence, see in the arrival and eventual settlement of the Norsemen a positive stimulus rather than a totally negative, destructive force. It is certainly true that, well before the first Viking raid, monasteries and church property were subject to attack, devastation and plundering by the Irish themselves in internecine feuds and even in feuds between rival monasteries. However these were almost ritual attacks, usually punitive reprisals, and it seems unlikely that they caused the same terror as the Viking raids.

The sight of the Viking ships coming up the Shannon must surely have been more fearful to the monks at Clonmacnoise than when they were attacked by the monks of Birr with whom they fought in 763, or the monks of Durrow in 806. The annals record plunder or attack by the Norsemen at Clonmacnoise, for example, in 834, 841, 844, 921, 935, 941, 945 and 1013, and plunder or attack on the monastery by the Irish in 832, 844, 934, 958, 960, 1023, 1044, 1050, 1060, 1065, 1077, several times in the 1080s and 1090s and in the twelfth century; in 952 Clonmacnoise was plundered by a joint party of Norse and Irish.

By the end of the eleventh century, when the Norsemen had founded Ireland's first towns – Dublin, Wexford, Waterford and Limerick – the Scandinavian influence can be found in Irish artefacts from other parts of the country. The Urnes style, for example, can be seen on the Shrine of St Patrick's Bell, made between 1094 and 1105. The superb crozier made about the same time for the Abbot of Clonmacnoise

Detail of a Viking sword inscribed HILTIPREHT. *It is made of iron and was found in a crannog at Ballinderry, County Westmeath.*

is partly carved in the earlier Scandinavian Ringerike style. Zoomorphic decoration on twelfth-century Irish work also reveals the influence of Scandinavian animal art. The Cross of Cong, made in 1123, probably at Clonmacnoise, shows the Scandinavian influence in Irish workshops by that time. While the central rock crystal is reminiscent of earlier Irish decoration, the front is divided into small panels whose decoration derives from the Urnes style. The bronze panels are edged with bands of silver, glass studs and niello. At the base of the cross, where it is joined to the shaft, it fits into the mouth of a dragon-like animal with blue glass eyes.

As the Norsemen eventually settled in increasing numbers they made contacts with the Irish at all levels of society. The northerners captured Irish men and women and kept them as slaves; the Irish, when they were successful, made slaves of Norse men and women. The Norse and the Irish mixed and intermarried. Olaf, the Norse King of Dublin who accepted Christianity and died on a pilgrimage to Iona, married an Irish princess, Gormflaith; after his death she married the Irish High King Brian Bóru, who won the final victory over the Norse at the Battle of Clontarf in 1014. The next High King, Maelsachnaill II, married a daughter of King Olaf; King Sihtric of Dublin, Olaf's son and successor, married a daughter of Brian Bóru. With the acceptance of Christianity in the Norse settlements in the tenth century, a Hiberno-Norse population developed which eventually merged into Irish society.

We may conclude, therefore, that while the Viking attacks must at first have had a negative influence on the development of Irish civilization, eventually the Norse presence was not entirely a disadvantage, and that, especially after the founding of the port towns and the establishment of foreign trade connections, that presence actually provided an impetus.

The Norse dioceses in Ireland were under the jurisdiction of Canterbury, which resulted in a new channel of cultural exchange between Ireland and other countries through the foreign-educated Irish Benedictines and the foreign Benedictines who were appointed to the Norse sees. Gilla Patrick, the second Bishop of Dublin who died in 1084, had taken his vows under St Wulfstan at Worcester, which was a great intellectual centre. His successor, Donngus O'hAingli (Donogh O'Hanly), who died in 1095, had been trained at Canterbury, and his nephew, Samuel O'hAingli, who succeeded him as the fourth Bishop of Dublin and died in 1121, had been a monk in the monastery at St Albans. Malchus (born Mael-Iosa O'hAnmire), first Bishop of Waterford and in 1110 first Archbishop of Cashel, had started at Winchester. Gilbert or Giselbert, first Bishop of Limerick, was a friend of the great St Anselm, the Italian-born Archbishop of Canterbury. Gilbert had known Anselm at Rouen in Normandy, had apparently also been at Bec and had reputedly studied in Germany and in Rome.

It was this cosmopolitan Benedictine, Gilbert, who presided at the Synod of Rath Breasail which convened in 1110. King Muirchertach of Munster, the most important ruler present, was anxious for ecclesiastical reform in Ireland and had corresponded with St Anselm. King Muirchertach had international connections; one of his sons-in-law was Sigurd the Crusader, son of the King of Norway, another was a Norman knight in Wales, Arnulph de Montgomery. The Synod of Rath Breasail heralded a new era in the Irish Church and a *rapprochement* with Rome, confirmed by the Synod of Kells in 1152, at which the Italian Cardinal Paparo presided as Papal Legate, and by the energetic reformatory zeal of St Malachy who while serving as Archbishop of Armagh and Primate of Ireland went to Rome for consultations with the Pope in 1139.

It is not surprising, in view of these contacts, that new ideas in church architecture reached Ireland in the first half of the twelfth century and that the Romanesque style then made its Irish début.

Incised drawing on the plank of a ship found in a Hiberno-Norse post and wattle house, excavated in Christ Church Place, Dublin. It depicts a look-out man in a ship's rigging.

Hiberno-Romanesque architecture

At the beginning of the twelfth century there is evidence of a rather timid attempt by Irish church-builders to introduce some adornment in the form of carved decoration on door jambs and facings and in finely chiselled architraves. Round-headed windows appeared, and extensions were added to little single-chamber churches by breaking the plain rounded chancel arch in the east wall and adding a chancel.

There is evidence of building interest in various parts of the country in the second decade of the twelfth century, although there is no documentary evidence to date most of the early churches with Romanesque features. The abbey church of St Peter and St Paul at Armagh, of which nothing remains, was built about this time by Imhar O'Hagan and the 'great stone church' at Armagh was re-roofed in 1125.

In 1127 King Cormac Mac Carthy of Desmond, on his return to Cashel from a year of pilgrimage at Lismore, began work on a new church on the Rock. At Lismore the King had been with St Malachy and with the Benedictine Malchus, the first Archbishop of Cashel, and had undoubtedly met Benedictine and other monks who had been in France, Germany, England and Italy; some of them may actually have been involved in church-building. The church that King Cormac built, consecrated in 1134, bears his name, *Teampuill Cormaic* (Cormac's Chapel). It is a grand, elegant church on a miniature scale, the total internal length being only 46 ft 9 ins. The plan is cruciform, a little transept being formed by the towers on either side of the junction of the nave and chancel. The stone roof is steeply pitched in the earlier Irish tradition, and the builder seems to have intentionally stressed the disproportionate height of the church in relation to its length and width. It contains lavish sculptural ornamentation. Inside, the chancel arch, composed of four orders, has naturalistic human heads sculpted on its voussoirs; there is blind arcading on the north and south walls of both nave and chancel and on the altar recess in the east wall. Outside there are three storeys of blind arcading on the south wall beneath one storey with engaged columns supporting the eaves course, and blind arcading on the towers. The elaborate, deeply recessed and richly sculpted north door has a carved scene in its tympanum. Most of the elements in the decorative carving can be found in Anglo-Norman buildings. The chancel roof is rib-vaulted, a technique brought back to Europe after the crusades; it was first used in Europe at Durham Cathedral, whose choir was completed in 1093. Its use in Ireland within 40 years of its first appearance in Europe indicates the presence of at least one builder-architect who was aware of the latest architectural developments abroad.

Since Cashel was such an important ecclesiastical centre, King Cormac's ornate new building was seen by many. Within a few years it had spawned churches in other places which combined some of its architectural and decorative detail. One such church can be seen at Kilmalkedar in County Kerry; only the west front survives of another at Roscrea, County Tipperary; and at Freshford, County Kilkenny, only a doorway survives, incorporated in a much later building. The influence of Cormac's Chapel is revealed in the blind arcading of the west wall of the old cathedral at Ardfert, County Kerry, and in the ruined churches at Donaghmore, County Tipperary, and Killeshin, County Leix.

In 1140, only six years after the consecration of Cormac's Chapel, St Malachy started to build a church at Bangor whose plan was so radically different that it provoked adverse criticism locally when the foundations were laid. Malachy had just returned from a visit to Rome, in the course of which he had passed through England and stayed at Clairvaux in France with St Bernard, founder of the Cistercian order. Malachy would have seen many beautiful and opulent churches on his travels. At Bangor he was probably imitating some church he had seen abroad, and the surprised comments when the foundations were being laid indicate that he was attempting a building on the basilical plan.

Two years later, in 1142, St Malachy founded the first Cistercian monastery in Ireland, at Mellifont beside the River Boyne. In the following year St Bernard sent a French monk, Robert, to Mellifont from Clairvaux to assist in the building. It was consecrated with pomp in 1157, after Malachy's death. Unfortunately the early church has been destroyed so nothing is known of its decoration, but excavation has revealed a basilical plan, a long nave with aisles, and with a crypt beneath at the west end, three chapels on the east wall of each transept, and a chancel at the east end.

Throughout the second half of the twelfth century builders and masons in Ireland adopted and adapted the Romanesque style in places as far apart as Dublin; White Island in Lough Erne, County Fermanagh; Clonmacnoise, County Offaly; Clonkeen, County Limerick; Killaloe, County Clare; Wicklow town; and Glendalough, County Wicklow. The plan of the Cistercian buildings was dictated by the rules of the order. The churches of the daughter houses of Mellifont were built on the basilical plan, similar to that of the church of the mother house. Elsewhere the builders contented themselves and their patrons with small nave and chancel buildings, concentrating the ornamentation in handsome recessed doorways and chancel arches, of which the Nun's Church at Clonmacnoise, begun in 1172, is a fine example. It was built by Derbhorgaill, Queen of Breffny, whose husband had been killed in battle in that year. The nave measures 36 ft × 19 ft 6 ins, the chancel 14 ft 3 ins × 13 ft 10 ins. The west door is richly sculpted, the first order carved with recessed and beaded chevrons, the second with beasts' heads biting roll moulding, while the third has foliar decoration. Running chevrons which terminate in serpents' heads decorate the piers, and another serpent, its head to the north, its tail to the south, decorates the hood-moulding. The chancel arch, also of three orders, is carved with bold, deep chevrons, double chevrons and fantastic heads.

As the Irish masons became familiar with the Romanesque decorative style they

incorporated Celtic and Scandinavian elements such as interlace and animal ornament. This, combined with the plan and the steeply pitched roof, resulted in a style peculiar to Ireland; because it amalgamated vernacular with imported Romanesque elements, it is called Hiberno-Romanesque.

The Hiberno-Romanesque style reached its zenith in the 1160s, and Clonfert Cathedral, County Galway, built in 1164, was its crowning achievement. This beautiful building was no exception to the Irish tradition of small churches; although a cathedral, it is only 82 ft in length. The marvellous west door, carved in brown sandstone, did not originally have its present innermost limestone arch-ring. The five original arch-rings, supported by alternating octagonal and cylindrical columns flanked by pilasters, are riotously ornamented with palmettes, dogs' heads biting arris moulding, rosettes, cable moulding, and circular bosses in high relief. In a steeply inclined pediment above the arches is a blind arcade with a human head carved under each arch, and above, at the top, in alternating raised and recessed panels, are human heads in rows of four, three, two, and one, reaching to the apex of the pediment. If Clonfert has the most splendid west door, the prize for the most splendid chancel arch must go to the Cathedral of Tuam, also in County Galway, where a superb arch survives in the nineteenth-century building. Spanning 16 ft, it is composed of five orders, each of its arch-rings supported by a pair of columns and each ring richly sculpted.

Crucifixion scenes

A bronze plaque found at Rinnagan, near Athlone, once gilded and probably originally the front of a book cover, depicts a bold crucifixion scene. Judging by

the mass of Celtic spirals and the bands of interlace which decorate the figures, it is a work of the late eighth century. Cherubim flank the upper part of the cross, while below, to either side, stand the Roman soldiers Stephaton and Longinus, portrayed like figures in contemporary manuscript decoration.

A crucifixion plaque from Clonmacnoise has the same composition although it is a much later work, probably dating from the eleventh century or possibly the twelfth. In this plaque classical influence is evident. The bearded Christ wears a chasuble decorated with an acanthus leaf pattern, while Stephaton with his sponge and Longinus with his spear wear tunics.

In the twelfth century the multiple biblical scenes of the earlier, higher crosses are replaced by the figure of the crucified Christ on the cross and the figure of a crozier-bearing bishop on the shaft. Here the work of the sculptor may reflect the twelfth-century reform movement in the Church in Ireland and the re-establishment of episcopal administration. Examples may be seen at Cashel, and at Tuam, County Galway, both episcopal seats, and at Dysert O'Dea in County Clare.

Towards the end of the twelfth century Celtic Christian Ireland was being drawn more closely into the orbit of Rome; it was affected by doctrinal and administrative reform within the Church, by the culture brought by clerics from England and France, by the increase in trade contacts with other European countries, and by increasing communication with the outside world. Celtic Ireland had absorbed and assimilated the Norse invaders, but it was totally unprepared for the arrival of ambitious knights who looked covetously at Irish land from across the Irish Sea.

3 The Lordship of Ireland

Laudabiliter

The Normans, who had made a successful leap across the English Channel from northern France in 1066 and conquered England, began 90 years later to consider extending their authority to Ireland. An English Cistercian monk, Nicholas Breakspear, himself the son of a monk of the monastery of St Albans, was elected to the papal throne in 1154 as Adrian IV. On Breakspear's succession to the papacy the Norman King of England, Henry II, sent an embassy to Rome to congratulate him. The King's envoys were charged with a second mission, to put before the Pope the King's desire to bring the Irish people fully into the orbit and jurisdiction of Rome. This, of course, he intended to accomplish by taking over Ireland himself.

As a cardinal, Adrian IV had been sent to Scandinavia to strengthen the connections of the northern kingdoms with the Holy See. He was an energetic, astute, tenacious man and there is no reason to doubt his sincerity in acceding to Henry II's request. Despite the reform movement of the twelfth century and the Synod of Kells in 1152, which outlawed concubinage and uncanonical unions and conferred the pallium on four archbishops – Armagh, Cashel, Dublin and Tuam – Ireland still did not conform to the French or Roman pattern of private morality and ecclesiastical discipline. Nor had the canon law of the church displaced the Brehon laws in all matters of legislation where the two disagreed.

Undoubtedly reports of Irish affairs which reached Rome from the papal representative in Ireland, Giolla Criost O Conairche, the Cistercian Bishop of Lismore, may have conveyed an alarming picture of Irish morality: in the interminable feuds and power struggles brutal murder, even fratricide, rape, blinding, maiming and plunder were frequent occurrences, while the matrimonial misconduct of the lusty rulers was flagrant.

The Pope's motives, therefore, may have been sincere, but unquestionably the King's motives were merely acquisitive. The Pope, relying on the Donation of Constantine, whereby the Holy See claimed all islands converted to Christianity, provided the English monarch with a papal bull, *Laudabiliter*. This authorized him to invade and conquer Ireland and hold the county as a fief of the Holy See provided that he enforced the payment of Peter's Pence, and instituted reforms to put an end to the 'enormous disorders and unchristian practices in that island'.

The bull was issued in 1155 but King Henry bided his time; he placed the precious document in his archives at Winchester and waited for a propitious moment. Eventually the opportunity was provided by a situation which arose from the internecine struggle between the Irish rulers themselves.

OPPOSITE *Cahir Castle.*

King Dermot of Leinster

Dermot Mac Murrough, the third son of Donnchadh Mac Murrough, King of Leinster and the Foreigners, was born in 1110. After the murder of his elder brother

51

he was elected to succeed to the throne of Leinster at the age of 16. He became over-ruler of an area which covered roughly the south-east quarter of Ireland, a region which had the closest and most frequent contacts with Britain and the Continent and which included jurisdiction over the 'foreigners', the inhabitants of the Hiberno-Norse towns of Dublin, Wexford, Wicklow and Arklow. In a time and place in which fickle alliances, fragile loyalties, treachery and violent revenge were the order of the day, King Dermot became deeply embroiled in a bitter power struggle which ended in the Norman King of England establishing his sovereignty over the Irish rulers.

King Dermot's controversial life-style mirrors the character of twelfth-century Irish society, at once pious and ruthless. He founded monasteries, among others the Cistercian Abbey at Baltinglass in 1148, the Augustinian Abbey at Ferns in 1158, and All Saints Priory in Dublin for the Augustinians in 1161. However, when a woman from the rival MacFaelain family was appointed Abbess at Kildare he had her abducted and raped, and replaced her by one of his own kinswomen. He contracted marriages in accordance with the native Brehon laws rather than Roman canon law. In the lifetime of his first wife, a sister of St Laurence O'Toole, the Abbot of Glendalough and later Archbishop of Dublin, he took a second wife, a niece of the raped Abbess of Kildare. According to custom, the junior wife made her obeisance to the senior wife and both lived at Ferns raising children to their royal husband. Then in 1152 Dermot abducted Derbhorgaill, the 44-year-old Queen of Breffny, two years his senior and married to his great enemy Tiernan O'Rourke, the ruler of Breffny. Despite the fact that Derbhorgaill screamed loudly when Dermot

Late thirteenth-century seal of Brian, King of Cenel-Eoghain (the present county of Tyrone) using his title in the inscription: 'Sigillum Brien Regis De Keneleogian'.

seized her, it appears that she had connived at the abduction by sending a message to Dermot through her brother the King of Meath, announcing that she had repudiated her husband. Such a repudiation would have been recognized under Brehon law as long as the abandoned husband received an honour-price for his wife, but Dermot took the lady, her cattle and chattels back to Ferns and refused to pay anything. This was a bad beginning for the moral reform promulgated by the Synod of Kells that year, and it heralded a reversal in King Dermot's fortunes. Derbhorgaill only shared the King of Leinster's bed for a year before returning with her cattle and chattels to Breffny and her cuckolded husband. The indignant King of Breffny demanded redress. Because Dermot refused everyone turned against him. In a powerful alliance with Rory O'Conor, the High King of Ireland, the ruler of Breffny swept down into Leinster. The odds were against Dermot; he was toppled from his throne.

The defeated monarch first consulted the papal representative, the Bishop of Lismore, and then slipped quietly off to England to seek help in regaining his realm. If he did not know already of the existence of the bull *Laudabiliter*, he would have learned of it at Lismore. From England he went to France to reach King Henry at his court at Acquitaine. In reply to the deposed Irish ruler's plea for help the English monarch received him as his vassal and liege-man and promised royal favour to any who should help Dermot to recover his state.

The mercenaries

In south-west Wales Dermot found the men to help him. Most of them were sons, grandsons and other relatives of the Welsh Princess Nesta who had borne sons not only to her husband, Gerald of Windsor, the Norman Constable of Pembroke Castle, but also to several lovers, including King Henry I and the Constable of Cardigan Castle. Two of Nesta's sons, Maurice FitzGerald and Robert FitzStephen, and her grandsons, Raymond Le Gros, William FitzMaurice, Milo FitzDavid (the son of the Bishop of St Davids), Meiler FitzHenry and Robert and Philip de Barry, had prominent roles in the conquest of Ireland. Another grandson, Gerald de Barry, remembered as Giraldus Cambrensis, was the chronicler of the Norman takeover, and a grand-daughter, Nesta, was the wife of Hervey de Mount Maurice (Montmorency), another prominent figure in the conquest of Ireland, and the uncle of Richard de Clare, Earl of Strigul and Pembroke, best known as Strongbow, the most important mercenary recruited by King Dermot. To secure Strongbow's services Dermot offered him in marriage his own daughter Aoife (Eva) with the promise of succession to the kingdom of Leinster on his death, a promise that Dermot could hardly have believed could be fulfilled because succession to the kingship was by election within the ruler's own family group. To lure Robert FitzStephen and Maurice FitzGerald to Ireland, Dermot promised them the town of Wexford as soon as these could take it. In addition Dermot engaged the services of footloose Flemish refugees who were stranded in Wales; a party of these able soldiers, knights, sergeants and archers under the leadership of Richard FitzGodebert de Roche accompanied the Irish ruler when he returned to reclaim his kingdom in the summer of 1167.

From the leaders of the Flemish mercenaries, Richard FitzGodebert de Roche and Maurice de Prendergast, descend the Roche and Prendergast families still numerous in Ireland today. From Maurice FitzGerald descend the Fitzgerald and Fitzmaurice families, including the illustrious Earls of Kildare (subsequently Dukes of Leinster), the Earls of Desmond and the Barons of Kerry. Strongbow in fact married the Princess of Leinster, and other prominent Normans also married into Irish ruling families: Hugh de Lacy married a Princess of Connacht, daughter of the High King of Ireland; William FitzAldhelm de Burgh, ancestor of the de Burghs or Burkes, married a daughter of Donal Mor O'Brien, King of Thomond.

The conquest   On his return Dermot at first feigned acceptance of his reduced status and paid the long overdue honour-price for Derbhorgaill – 100 ounces of gold. However, when Robert FitzStephen landed at Bannow in County Wexford in May 1169, with a contingent of about 500 men including 60 horsemen and 300 archers, the recovery of Leinster by military force began with the capture of Wexford town. In 1170 Dermot took Dublin, and in that summer Strongbow landed in Ireland with 200 knights and 1,000 soldiers. Despite their inferiority in numbers the mail-clad, helmeted Norman mercenaries enjoyed superiority over the Irish in military tactics, equipment, training and technology. The Irish horsemen still went into battle bareback, without armour; their foot soldiers wielded cumbersome axes.

By the time of King Dermot's death at Ferns in May 1171 not only was Leinster in the hands of the rapacious Norman mercenaries but, egged on by Dermot, they had thrust well beyond its frontiers. Fearful that the ambitious barons, Strongbow in particular, might well claim territories independent of the crown, King Henry considered it wise to proceed to Ireland and assert his own sovereignty.

The King received Strongbow's homage and conferred with the papal representative, the Bishop of Lismore, requesting that a synod be convened at Cashel to legislate on matters of moral teaching and diocesan and parochial administration to bring the Irish church more closely into line with Rome. By so doing the King must have intended to convince the Pope of his good intentions regarding the terms of *Laudabiliter* and to help placate the Pope's wrath over the murder of Thomas à Becket. At Cashel all the bishops of Ireland put their seal to their recognition of King Henry as overlord of their country. The King also received the submission of many of the Irish rulers, and renewals of allegiance from his invader barons. In October 1175 peace was concluded between the English King and the High King of Ireland. By the terms of the Treaty of Windsor the High King swore fealty to Henry and became his vassal, holding his own realm of Connacht directly from the English crown. Henry II recognized the High King's overlordship of all the Irish save those living under Anglo-Norman lords. Broadly this arrangement suited both parties. A powerful, but not too powerful, high king in Ireland was a bulwark for the English king against the power of any over-ambitious barons, while English recognition of his overlordship of the Irish bolstered the High King's authority over the fractious Irish monarchs, especially the ruler of Thomond.

In the wake of the land-hungry barons and their knights came the rank and file of their soldiery; the spoils were distributed among them. Following the bigger fry came Anglo-Norman freebooters. Other immigrants came from England to settle, including farmers, civil servants and tradesmen. Where the Anglo-Normans incorporated towns they did so on the model of Breteuil in Normandy, delineating the status and rights of the burgesses in the same manner.

The allocation to the Anglo-Normans of the kingdom of Meath, the realm of the O Maoil Seachlainn kings which was granted as a fief to Hugh de Lacy, typifies the programme of resettlement. De Lacy divided up his rich new fief among his principal officers, men whose names we can still find today among their descendants in that same region, such as Tuite, Cusack (de Cussac), Nugent (de Nogent), Fleming, Cruise (de Cruys), and Plunket. These men further parcelled out their shares among their own henchmen, who in turn placed tenants on their land. Thus western European feudal practice was introduced to Ireland and manorial holdings were founded, similar to those in Wales and England. Fortifications were erected to hold and defend the earldom; at its *caput*, Trim, an important castle was built. In 1202 the seat of the episcopal see was moved to Newtown Trim, a mile from the castle. An Anglo-Norman, Simon de Rochfort, was appointed bishop; in 1206 he founded a cathedral there and brought Augustinians from Paris to serve it. Within 40 years of the invasion the local scene changed from Celtic Irish to Anglo-Norman.

The motte and bailey forts

To consolidate their positions the newcomers built strongholds, the first of which, of the kind depicted in the Bayeux tapestry, consisted of a great flat-topped earthen mound called a motte, on top of which was usually a timber tower surrounded by a palisade. Around the base of the motte was a D-shaped or U-shaped enclosure surrounded by a palisade and a ditch. At Knockgraffon, County Tipperary, the impressive earthwork of one of these mottes can still be seen; it was built in 1192 by Anglo-Normans advancing from Leinster into the kingdom of Thomond. At Granard, County Longford, are the remains of another great motte, said to be the biggest in Ireland. At Callan, County Kilkenny, where the town charter was granted in 1217 by Strongbow's son-in-law William, the Earl Marshal, there is a motte which would have defended the place. Mottes with well-preserved baileys may be seen in County Louth, at Dun Dealgan, a stronghold of the de Verdons, and Greenmount. The motte in the Ravernet Gap at Duneight, County Down, which protected a strategic position – the passage from the west into the Down plateau – was built on a much earlier Bronze Age burial site. At Holywood, County Down, there is a motte which may be the 'castle' of Holywood mentioned in 1234 as the *caput* of the de Sankeville manor. Other mottes may be seen at Ardmulchan, County Meath, dominating a stretch of the River Boyne; at Ardscull, County Kildare; and at Castleruddery, County Wicklow. The motte with a timber tower which Hugh de Lacy put up at Trim in 1172 had to be deliberately destroyed and the site temporarily abandoned in the following year when the Irish swept down on the conquerors of Meath.

The castles of the conquerors

Within a short time of their arrival the new magnates built more permanent strongholds, defensible stone-built castles with residential accommodation. John de Courcy had set out with 22 knights and 300 followers to conquer Ulidia, the part of the

The massive cylindrical keep of Dundrum, County Down, John de Courcy's castle dating from the early years of the invasion.

present province of Ulster between Newry and the Bann comprising County Down and County Antrim. He had been amazingly and speedily successful in his enterprise, soon routing the Ulidians and seizing their capital, Downpatrick. Following the Norman practice he built castles as he advanced and manned them with his own followers. In the 1180s he began building a stone keep on a rocky dyke jutting into the lough at Carrickfergus, County Antrim. The plan of the keep is rectangular; it is an unbuttressed four-storey tower, 55 × 60 ft, and 90 ft in height. De Courcy also started building a castle at Dundrum in County Down before he was overthrown by Hugh de Lacy in 1204. On a natural mound on a hill overlooking the plains of Lecale, the bay, and the pass between the Mourne Mountains and the foothills of Slieve Croob, stands the massive cylindrical keep, similar to the one built about 1200 at Pembroke by the Earls Marshal; a strong polygonal curtain wall encloses the ward.

When King Henry II wintered in Dublin in 1171 he contented himself with a royal dwelling of wattle-work constructed by his new Irish vassals. In 1204 King John ordered his justiciar, Meiler FitzHenry, to build a strong castle at Dublin with stout walls and good ditches. Meiler chose to build on the same ridge on which the Norse Kings of Dublin had had their fort, the site of the present Dublin Castle, which incorporates parts of the Anglo-Norman building. The castle was built with great towers protecting the angles of the curtain wall but without a keep within the ward. This was the plan of other castles built in towns about that time, such as Limerick Castle, completed by 1202, and Kilkenny Castle, built by William the Earl Marshal in 1204. At Dublin, the windows of the chapel built inside the walled bailey were glazed with stained glass in 1242; subsequently a detached hall was also built in the ward.

When King John visited Trim in 1210 it appears that the great stone castle there

LEFT *Carrickfergus Castle, County Antrim.*

BELOW *Trim Castle, County Meath.*

was not completed because he held court in a nearby meadow. The castle has a monumental rectangular keep with an unusual rectangular tower projecting on each side of its flanks. The keep stands in a large bailey of over three acres which is enclosed by a curtain wall with angle and lateral turrets and barbicans at both entrances. King John also stayed in 1210 at Carlingford Castle in County Louth, of which substantial vestiges survive, including thirteenth-century additions.

The ruins of a number of castles built by the first generation of Anglo-Normans can be seen today. Gerald FitzGerald's castle at Maynooth, County Kildare, was begun in 1203. Ferns Castle, whose ruins include thirteenth-century trefoil-headed windows, was built about 1200. Carlow Castle was built early in the thirteenth century. Other examples are Dunamase Castle, County Leix, now very ruinous, Adare Castle, County Limerick, the tall donjon of Nenagh Castle and Terryglass Castle, both in County Tipperary; both Nenagh and Terryglass were built before 1206 by Theobald FitzWalter, whom Henry II appointed Hereditary Chief Butler of Ireland, and who is the progenitor of the numerous Butler families in Ireland. Another relic which appears to date from the early thirteenth century is the cylindrical tower now joined to a later building and still inhabited as part of Leixlip Castle, above the Liffey in County Kildare. The ruined lower part of another tower of that period, with walls 11 ft thick, may be seen at Shanid in County Limerick; it was built on a motte and surrounded by a curtain wall.

The tall, multi-storeyed keep introduced to Ireland an entirely new concept of accommodation on several levels instead of spread out in a single storey. Stores, and sometimes domestic livestock, were kept on the ground floor and presumably guards watched there too. The principal chamber was on the first floor, usually reached by a narrow mural stair, sometimes by a timber stair. At night the guards slept in the first-floor chamber to protect the stair to the upper storeys, where the lord of the castle and his family slept.

New churches and cathedrals

At the Synod of Cashel, which Henry II had instigated on his arrival, the Irish hierarchy agreed that henceforth in Ireland the Divine Office should be celebrated as in England, according to the Use of Sarum. The synod also promulgated a new parochial system with newly delimited parishes for which churches were required. The Anglo-Norman lords of the new manors were generous in grants and endowments for churches which served their tenantry. The conquerors were also liberal in founding new monasteries manned with Anglo-Norman monks; they hoped to assure the well-being of their souls and, at the same time, the co-operation of a loyal ecclesiastical administration to play a vitally useful part in their colonial apparatus.

At New Ross, County Wexford, a boom town of the settlement, William, the Earl Marshal, and his wife, the heiress daughter of Strongbow and Aoife, built an aisled, cruciform parish church about 1210. Compared with the little Irish churches and even the twelfth-century Irish cathedrals, it was very large and magnificent. The Anglo-Norman nave and chancel parish church at Kinsale, County Cork, with an aisled nave and short north transept, is a simpler and smaller but still substantial building. Probably more typical of the parish churches of the settlement is the ruin of Cannistown church in County Meath. The nave has been rebuilt but the chancel, which has a fine arch and measures 24 × 15 ft, dates from the beginning of the thirteenth century.

It is in their cathedrals, especially the two in Dublin, and in the remains of the magnificent new abbeys, that one can best grasp the impression of power, elegance, wealth and culture that the Anglo-Normans must have conveyed. How awestruck the Irish must have been who looked at the soaring grandeur of the nave of Christ Church in Dublin or of St Patrick's and saw for the first time the dignity and wonder of a beautiful triforium and a clerestory.

OPPOSITE *St Patrick's Cathedral, Dublin. A view of the nave.*

The death in 1181 of St Laurence O'Toole, the Archbishop of Dublin and brother-in-law of King Dermot of Leinster, provided Henry II with the opportunity of appointing an Anglo-Norman prelate. He chose a man he had reason to trust, who had been a monk at Evesham but had never taken holy orders. His name was John Comyn and he had served the King faithfully as an emissary. Pope Lucius III obligingly ordained Comyn, consecrated him a bishop and gave him the pallium. Comyn's policy was to enhance and augment the importance of his office in the sphere of government and administration. So well did he achieve this that some of his successors came to exercise a role which rivalled that of the King's deputy in Ireland. In church affairs he strove to eradicate the obstinate vestiges of local Celtic usage in favour of Roman orthodoxy. At a provincial synod in 1186 he caused canons to be passed requiring stricter repression of irregularities still prevalent among Irish clerics. Moreover, by his legal acceptance of the archi-episcopal estates as a barony, Comyn marked a further step in the feudalization of Ireland.

Work began on Christ Church Cathedral in Dublin following Comyn's appointment. He was buried in the choir in 1212, the work being completed in 1240. The first phase of work on the choir and transepts was in the late Romanesque tradition. The nave and aisles, built in the second phase, were the first manifestation in Ireland of a pure Gothic style. The plan of Christ Church is based on that of west of England churches, near Evesham where Comyn had been a monk and in the area where he had served as itinerant justice, and the stone was brought from near Bristol. Roger Stalley's study of the richly carved capitals in the chancel and transepts has led him to conclude that the master mason was also brought from England, possibly from Glastonbury where there is similar work and where Comyn was Abbot before coming to Dublin, while the master mason of the second building phase came from Worcestershire.

In 1190 Archbishop Comyn ordered the demolition of an ancient church in Dublin dedicated to St Patrick. In its place he founded a non-monastic collegiate church and built his own palace in the vicinity. Comyn's successor, Archbishop Henry de Loundres, raised St Patrick's to the status of a cathedral. Building work began in the 1220s on a prestigious edifice which, like its neighbour and rival, Christ Church, looked to the west of England for its model.

The provincial Anglo-Norman cathedrals were not built on such a grand scale as the two in Dublin; although several of them boasted architectural distinction, none combined such Dublin features as a three-stage elevation, an ambulatory around the choir and a lofty, stone rib-vault. Not all were cruciform buildings. Waterford Cathedral, for example, demolished in the eighteenth century, was a long nave and chancel structure, as was Ardfert Cathedral whose long, gaunt shell survives. Kilkenny Cathedral is a fine example of the Gothic style in the provinces. Work began early in the thirteenth century and it was apparently completed in the 1260s. It has a broad, beautiful, aisled nave, the aisles continuing east of the transepts along a little more than half the length of the choir. As the cathedral had a timber roof the builder did not have to consider the problem of supporting a stone vault, so he was able to light the clerestory with large quatrefoil windows. The quatrefoil is the main decorative feature of the handsome west doorway, apparently the work of a talented master mason and sculptor who also worked on churches at Gowran and Thomastown in County Kilkenny. English influence reached cathedrals such as Killaloe, built in the first quarter of the century, and Limerick, founded by Domhnall Mor O'Brien, King of Thomond, which was built mainly in the last two decades of the twelfth century and finished by 1207. The cruciform building with an aisled nave and short chancel showed in its design the influence of the abbey churches of the Cistercians.

OPPOSITE *The Franciscan friary of Ross Errilly, County Galway.*

FOLLOWING PAGES
LEFT The Festival of St Kevin at the Seven Churches, Glendalough. *This painting by Joseph Peacock (1783–1837) records the animated annual assembly at Glendalough, a riotous communion of piety, gaiety and social intercourse. The event became so obstreperous that it was suppressed by the Catholic hierarchy.*

RIGHT *Bunratty Castle, County Clare, built in 1450 by Maccon Mac Sioda Macnamara and his son Sean Finn. It passed into the hands of the O'Briens, Princes and later Earls of Thomond. The castle has been restored by the Office of Public Works with financial assistance from Lord Gort, and is open to the public.*

RIGHT *Jerpoint Abbey, County Kilkenny. A view towards the west end of the abbey church.*

Abbeys

Thirteen or fourteen Cistercian abbeys had been founded in Ireland before the Anglo-Norman conquest. St Mary's Abbey at Dublin and Erinagh Abbey in County Down were daughter houses of Savigny in France; the others all derived from Mellifont. Of these the most prominent were Bective Abbey, County Meath; Boyle Abbey, County Roscommon; Monasternenagh, County Limerick; and Baltinglass Abbey, County Wicklow, all daughter houses of Mellifont, and Jerpoint Abbey, County Kilkenny, a daughter of Baltinglass; Inishlounaght Abbey in County Tipperary was a daughter house of Monasternenagh. As a group, the Cistercian abbeys were the most distinguished buildings in Ireland, varying in style but generally conforming to an arrangement around a central cloister, the church to the north, the chapter house with dormitory above to the east, the refectory and kitchen to the south, the quarters of the lay brothers to the west. Usually the church had a short east end, a long aisled nave in which a screen divided the lay brothers from the choir monks, and short transepts with east chapels. Under the Anglo-Normans building proceeded on some of the existing abbeys, and several important new foundations were made. John de Courcy and his wife founded Grey Abbey in 1193 with monks from Holme Cultram Abbey in England, and in 1187 Inch Abbey, also in County Down, with monks from the English abbey of Furness in Lancashire. Hervey de Mount Maurice (Montmorency), the uncle of Strongbow and steward of his Irish estates, founded Dunbrody Abbey in County Wexford in 1180 or 1182; Strongbow's son-in-law, William the Earl Marshal, founded Tintern Abbey, County Wexford, in 1200 with monks from Tintern Abbey in Wales, and he founded Graiguenamanagh Abbey, County Kilkenny, in 1207 with monks from Stanley Abbey in England.

There are substantial and beautiful remains of several of these abbeys, and they merit inspection because the visitor can still gain a vivid impression of their former splendour and importance. Some will find Dunbrody the most attractive, magnificently situated beside the estuary of the Suir; most of its imposing ruins date from the thirteenth century. At Mellifont the most impressive sight is the lavabo, an octagonal two-storey building in the Romanesque style, where the monks washed before going into the refectory; it was built about 1200. The ruins of Jerpoint Abbey are undeniably beautiful, especially when the sun highlights the

OPPOSITE *St Kevin's Kitchen, Glendalough, County Wicklow. This little Early Christian church is known as St Kevin's Kitchen because of the chimney-like round tower, which does not adjoin the building but rises from its traditional Irish chambered roof.*

The vaulted chancel of the Cistercian abbey church at Knockmoy, County Galway.

decorative detail on the capitals in the nave and lights the charming cloister, built in the fifteenth century but probably modelled on an earlier one. Both Grey Abbey, which has a handsome west doorway, and Inch were constructed from the outset in the Gothic style.

Boyle Abbey in County Roscommon, although the foundation of an Irish monarch and situated in Irish territory, exhibits in its architecture notable English influence such as early English lancet windows and clusters of triple shafts – thirteenth-century work. There are substantial remains of two other Cistercian abbeys in Irish territory: Knockmoy Abbey, County Galway, a daughter of Boyle founded by the King of Connacht in 1190, and Corcomroe Abbey, County Clare, a daughter of Inishlounaght, founded by the O'Briens of Thomond. The church of Corcomroe Abbey, built about 1200, is 135 ft long, 25 ft wide and 50 ft across the transepts; this is modest in size compared with the usual length of the Cistercian abbey churches which was around 200 ft.

The Cistercians have left the grandest remains, but there were other monastic orders introduced from the Continent to Ireland. The Augustinians, who came to Ireland after St Malachy's visit to Arrouaise in 1139, in fact had closer contact with the people than the rather aristocratic Cistercians. They too built some splendid churches and abbeys or priories, more varied in plan than those of the Cistercians because their arrangement was not dictated by their rule.

One fine example of an early thirteenth-century Augustinian building is at Cong, County Mayo, where the elaborately carved capitals of the slype doorway of the priory alone merit a visit. At Killone in County Clare are the remains of an Augustinian nunnery beside a lake with interesting thirteenth-century windows of three architectural styles – Romanesque, Transitional and Early Gothic – indicating that fashions penetrated more slowly and haphazardly to the Gaelic west. Probably the best-known early Augustinian church is the one at Ballintubber, County Mayo, because it has been restored and is used. It gives a good impression of what a large and richly endowed early thirteenth-century church was like.

While Cong, Killone and Ballintubber were all Irish foundations, founded by kings of Connacht and Thomond, the magnificent ruined priory at Athassel in County Tipperary was founded for the Augustinians by the Anglo-Norman William de Burgh, who died in 1205 and whose son was buried there in 1208. It is a vast complex with extensive domestic buildings. The cruciform church, 210 ft in length, has a beautiful door in the screen dividing the nave and choir; five tall, slender lancet windows in the choir convey an impression of the building's former elegance.

Benedictines from England and France, Premonstratensians from France and Knights Templar were all active in Ireland in the years following the Anglo-Norman conquest. Also energetic in thirteenth-century ecclesiastical life, particularly in pastoral activities, were the mendicant Franciscans, the Dominicans who were in Ireland by 1224, only three years after the death of their founder, and the Carmelites who came about 1260. Nothing remains of the 24 early Carmelite foundations, and most of the early Franciscan buildings have vanished or been altered, but at Ardfert, County Kerry, is the ruin of an imposing Franciscan church built in the 1260s and modelled on the nearby cathedral. The five-light east window of Ennis Friary in County Clare dates from the thirteenth century when it was founded. In the town of Sligo can be seen the shell of the handsome church of the Dominicans, whose friary there was founded by Maurice FitzGerald, Justiciar of Ireland, in 1252.

By the end of the thirteenth century and in the fourteenth a simple Early Gothic style was usually adopted by Irish church-builders. The Bruce invasion in 1315, when the Scots king, at the invitation of the Ulster chiefs, ravaged parts of Ireland in a bold attempt to seize the crown, must have been a deterrent to building projects. Even more efficient were the ravages of the Black Death, which reached Ireland about the middle of the century, taking an enormous toll of life. No particularly Irish interpretation of Gothic developed as it had in the case of Romanesque, although distinctive characteristics did appear, such as the stepped parapet, which had not come from England. The model for a stepped parapet may have been seen by an Irish builder in the Pyrenees, where it occurs on both the French and Spanish sides. It was used on Kildare and Cashel cathedrals and on Gowran parish church in County Kilkenny. But while the architects had not evolved an Irish style, many of the settlers had adopted Irish customs and manners.

The east end of the Franciscan friary church at Ardfert, County Kerry.

Racial laws

By the mid-fourteenth century the process of assimilation of Anglo-Norman and English settlers generally had reached a point where it caused concern to the government. In 1366 Lionel, Duke of Clarence, son of King Edward III and his father's deputy in Ireland, summoned a parliament at Kilkenny which took measures to halt this. The preamble of the legislation passed by that parliament states clearly what was happening:

> Whereas at the conquest of the land of Ireland and for a long time after the English of the said land used the English language, mode of riding and apparel and were governed and ruled ... by the English law ... now many English of the said land, forsaking the English language, fashion, mode of riding, laws and usages, live and govern themselves according to the manners, fashion and language of the Irish enemies, and also have made divers marriages and alliances between themselves and the Irish enemies....

Hoping to remedy this state of affairs, which undermined the English authority, the parliament of 1366 passed the Statutes of Kilkenny, which forbade alliance by marriage, concubinage, or by the Irish practice of fosterage, forbade the presentation of Irish clerics to a cathedral or collegiate church, forbade the English to receive Irish minstrels or other entertainers, forbade the English to speak Irish, to ride or to dress according to the Irish fashion, and insisted on the separation of English and Irish religious. English monasteries were forbidden to accept or profess Irish postulants. Hurling, a game still popular in Ireland, was forbidden for the English living on the Marches, the border between the English and Irish lands. The reason given was that it caused 'great evils and maims', thus weakening the border defences. It was, of course, easier to make such laws than to implement them, but what is interesting is the state of affairs which they expose and the intentions of the legislators. The efforts of the crown were unsuccessful. At the beginning of the fifteenth century the King's writ was only enforced in the walled towns and in a strip of land along the east coast, the 'Pale'.

The Pale An identifiable Pale emerged by the mid-fifteenth century covering parts of the counties of Dublin, Meath, Kildare and Louth, where the English interest was paramount. The extent of the English Pale varied from time to time according to the success of incursions, which came especially from the Irish on its borders, like the fierce O'Tooles and O'Byrnes in Wicklow. Fortifications were built to protect the Pale. In 1495 an act of parliament provided for a ditch to be built along the frontiers of the shrunken Pale; a recommended size for castles was published.

Fortified houses A fortified residential tower which conformed to these specifications may still be seen at Donore, County Meath. Roodstown Castle in County Louth is another example of such a fortified residence built in the fifteenth century. It is built on four storeys with two projecting turrets, one of which contains the stair and the other the latrine (garde-robe) and some small chambers. The three-, four-, or five-storey rectangular tower found widespread favour as a defensible residence. These tower-houses were built not only in the Pale and on the lands of the great landlords of Anglo-Norman descent outside the Pale, like the Butlers of Ormonde and the Fitzgeralds of Desmond, but also, eventually, by some of the Irish in the fifteenth, sixteenth and seventeenth centuries. About 400 were built in County Limerick alone, about 300 in County Cork, between 200 and 300 in County Tipperary, County Clare and County Galway. The ruined, creeper-clad tower-house is a frequent landmark on the Irish landscape today.

Churches in vulnerable places in the Pale and the Marches were sometimes built with fortifications. The fifteenth-century church at Newcastle, County Dublin, had a three-storey fortified tower at its west end. Another example, with a four-storey battlemented residential tower, may be seen at Taghmon in County Westmeath.

The great magnates built castles on a grander scale, like the Earls of Desmond's Askeaton Castle in County Limerick, with a 90 ft high keep and an elegant detached banqueting hall, 72 × 31 ft, and their other seat at Newcastle West in the same county. Also dating from the fifteenth century, and so strong that it was long considered impregnable, is Cahir Castle in County Tipperary, a stronghold of one branch of the powerful Butler family. This splendid feudal seat has three wards, outer, middle and inner. The residence of the Barons of Cahir was a stout keep in the innermost ward, and a detached great hall for audiences and banquets was added in the sixteenth century. The entrance to the inner ward was protected by a tower flanking the gate, a portcullis fitted in the gate, and a machicoulis on the wall above. Cahir Castle has undergone little change in nearly 400 years.

Gaelic society The less fertile lands in the Gaelic west offered much less attraction to settlers. The Irish outside the Pale were considered a separate nation by the English authorities; no objections were raised to the Irish rulers there administering justice according to their own statutes, which were rooted in Brehon law. Hereditary jurists advised the individual rulers by whom they were appointed or recognized. The great magnates of Anglo-Norman origin who administered justice in their own territories, as did the Earls of Ormonde, also consulted the hereditary Brehons in formulating legislature. On the Marches a hybrid legal system obtained, part Brehon, part English. In Galway Roman law was adopted.

The customs of earlier Celtic society persisted. The family corporation remained the unit of land ownership, the method of partition of the land varying from family to family and from place to place. Most of the population endured a miserably low status as tenants of the landowning families in conditions close to serfdom.

Sexual permissiveness was the order of the day. Secular marriage was still the norm, despite centuries of Christianity, synods, and canons; divorce was easy, and a succession of spouses frequent. No outward formal ceremony was necessary to validate a marriage; the Christian matrimonial ceremony was rare. The Anglo-Normans who 'went Irish' followed this easy-going matrimonial practice. Richard de Burgo (Burke), second Earl of Clanrickarde, as late as 1582 left four living wives at his death. An ecclesiastical dispensation was, however, required for consanguineous unions, and a great number of Irish marriages, being between kin, fell into this category; only the rich troubled to apply, however, and only after the birth of children. A curious custom persisted by which a mother could transfer her child at any time to another father merely by declaring that he and not her husband had sired the child. Church synods of 1453 and 1502 sought to put an end to this practice but without success. The ancient custom of fosterage also continued.

As well as the hereditary jurists, of whom prominent examples were the Mac Egans in Ormond, the Mac Clancys in Thomond and the O'Breslins in Fermanagh, there were many other hereditary professions. Of these the poets were held in the highest regard. There were hereditary historians, who were sometimes also poets, and hereditary musicians, and there were also hereditary physicians, like the O'Hickey family which originated in Clare and whose name comes from the Irish *iceadh*, meaning healer. At the head of each profession in a given territory was the *ollamh*, appointed or at least recognized by the ruler.

The first Anglo-Norman settlers found little to praise in the Irish except the skill of their musicians. Giraldus Cambrensis wrote of the 'rapid fingerwork' of the Irish harpers, their 'unfailingly disciplined art', their 'ornate rhythms and profusely intricate polyphony'. Irish harpers provided music for the crusaders. The hereditary musicians maintained their art throughout the Middle Ages, and their expertise was recognized in Renaissance Italy. The beautiful medieval Irish harp in Trinity College, Dublin, dates from the fourteenth century; its soundbox is carved from a solid piece of willow, according to the traditional Irish method.

The poets, now generally referred to as bards, eulogized the person, the ancestry, and the deeds of their patrons. Their compositions, read by a professional reciter to the accompaniment of a harper, spurred the listeners to heroic action. For this reason the English authorities considered that the poets incited violence and rebellion. The strict bardic tradition founded on rigid training and technique lasted from the thirteenth century into the seventeenth. Gerald FitzGerald, the Gaelicized Anglo-Norman Earl of Desmond, who died in 1398, adopted the Irish bardic traditions and wrote in Irish. The most popular poem in Ireland for much of that time was a composition by the fourteenth-century poet Gofraidh Fionn O'Dalaigh. It relates the experience of a child born and raised in a dark prison cell who poignantly asks his mother, 'Is there another world,/Brighter than where we are,/A home more lovely than this?'

The military force of an Irish ruler included horsemen, infantry and axe-wielding

Tower house at Belvelly, County Cork.

ABOVE *Quin Friary, County Clare.*

LEFT *A medieval harp,
misleadingly known as Brian
Boru's harp.*

mercenaries. The Irish horsemen spurned stirrups which had been in use elsewhere in western Europe for a thousand years. Carrying a javelin, a sword and a dagger, the Irish rode on a cushion attached with a breast strap and used a snaffle rather than a bit. The salaried foot soldiers or kerne (who wore no armour) were noted for their fleetfootedness. The mercenaries, families who came to Ireland from western Scotland like the Mac Sweenys, Mac Donnells and Mac Dowells, hired out their services where they were needed. Known as galloglass, they wore a coat of mail and fought fiercely with a heavy, long-handled axe.

The hereditary nature of the professions in Ireland extended to the Church. By the end of the thirteenth century celibacy had been accepted as the rule, but many clerics continued to raise families. According to canon law the sons of the clergy were illegitimate and could not hold ecclesiastical office without a papal dispensation; but the ready sale of these in the fourteenth century permitted the continuation of hereditary offices in the Irish Church. A fourteenth-century Archbishop of Cashel of the O'Grady family fathered an Archbishop of Tuam, who in turn fathered a Bishop of Elphin whose descendants held ecclesiastical offices in the sixteenth century. Murtough O'Kelly, Archbishop of Tuam, who died in 1407, had three sons

in holy orders; one succeeded him as Bishop of Clonfert, was eventually promoted to his father's Archbishopric and fathered a rector and an archdeacon; Archbishop O'Kelly's youngest son became Abbot of Knockmoy. There seems to have been no social disgrace attached to clerical marriages and their issue. Two fourteenth-century bishops of Raphoe married rulers' daughters; a fifteenth-century Archdeacon of Clogher enjoyed more than half a century of clerical marriage with the daughter of the Bishop of Clogher and left a large family, of whom one son also became Bishop of Clogher and many descendants filled important ecclesiastical offices. As late as the mid-sixteenth century Turlough O'Brien, Bishop of Killaloe (son of a Bishop of Kilmacdaugh and grandson of a former Bishop of Killaloe), married a daughter of the Earl of Thomond.

By the fifteenth century the monasteries had become secularized. The clergy largely adopted the lay dress of knee-length tunics and great cloaks, wore long hair and grew long moustaches in the Irish fashion.

Visitors to medieval Ireland commented on the near nakedness of the Irish masses, whose poor clothing, a blanket-like cloak, often did not cover the genitals. It seems that only the mendicant friars, continuing to preach the Christian message, were exempt from the generally low standards. They were prolific builders, mostly in rural areas. Ninety new friaries were built in the fifteenth century, over two-thirds of them Franciscan foundations. The ruins of a number of their fine churches survive; notable are those of Rosserk and Moyne Friaries, County Mayo, and Claregalway Friary, County Galway, built in the fifteenth century by the popular and influential Franciscans. Of the same period is the Dominican Friary at Burrishoole, County Mayo. These churches had a section in the nave reserved for the laity; usually a belfry tower was built over the partition wall of the nave and choir. Close to the church were the claustral buildings, usually with an upper storey over the ambulatory of the cloister.

Art and craftsmanship

Painting in Ireland lagged so far behind Continental art that it would be ridiculous even to consider it in the same terms as the art of the Italian *trecento*, *quattrocento* or *cinquecento*. Even though some painting may have perished at the hands of the iconoclasts of the Reformation, it seems unlikely that there was ever much in medieval Ireland. The very little which survives is primitive, uninspired work. The artist-scribes who illuminated the *Book of Ballymote* in the fourteenth century, for instance, fell far below the standard of their Celtic Christian predecessors. The medieval illuminators used the beautiful earlier books for ideas but their work is unimaginative and blandly derivative, a far cry from the vigour and intricate love-liness of the models. In Holy Cross Abbey, County Tipperary, is a fresco with a secular subject, a primitively executed hunting scene. Other churches may have had simple frescoes but few survive. Frescoes depicting the Three Live Kings and the Three Dead Kings in the chancel of Knockmoy Abbey, County Galway, another Cistercian foundation, are barely visible. The Knockmoy Cistercians established a cell on Clare Island which may account for frescoes in the chancel of a church there which depict St Michael the Archangel with the scales of Judgment, other figures and animals.

Wood carvings may also have perished at the hands of the iconoclasts but the surviving statuary is stiff and, were it not for its rarity, uninteresting. Exceptions are the beautifully carved harps such as the one in Trinity College, delicately decorated with interlacing and other Celtic motifs and with a rock crystal set in its silver finial; and the misericords in Limerick Cathedral. Unique in Ireland, these beautifully carved choir stalls, made about 1480, are richly decorated with figures from medieval bestiaries – the manticore, the wyvern, the griffin, the amphisboena and the lindworm.

The book shrine of the Cathach of St Columba.

Metalworkers also drew inspiration from the bestiaries, as can be seen from the silver-gilt shrine made for St Seanan's bell in the fourteenth century. Examples of medieval metalwork are rare. Many beautiful and precious objects have probably been lost, melted down, or otherwise destroyed; the rich treasury of offerings and ex-votos of Our Lady of Trim and the revered effigy itself were sacked and destroyed at the Reformation. Even Ireland's holiest relic, the ancient Baculum Jesu, was a victim of iconoclastic fervour. The few masterpieces which survive testify to the talent of the metalworkers, craftsmen such as John O'Barrden who made a silver-gilt book shrine with repoussé figures of saints, and the silversmith who worked on the shrine of the Cathach of St Columba about 1400. It has a central figure of Christ, his hand raised in blessing, flanked by a bishop giving benediction, and a crucifixion scene. A silver-gilt crozier with coloured enamel decoration, and a leather mitre with silver-gilt plaques encrusted with gems and pearls, made in 1418 for the Bishop of Limerick, are pieces of the highest quality. Thomas O'Carryd, who made the mitre, was probably also the maker of the elaborate crozier which has free-standing figures of the Blessed Virgin, the Trinity, St Peter, St Paul, St Patrick and St Munchin. Images of other saints are engraved on silver-gilt plates with an enamel background, and there is a delightful Annunciation scene in the crocketed crook. The surname O'Carryd, if it ever existed, has disappeared. (Perhaps the signature should be read as O'Carryl?) Presumably this craftsman was Irish. He was well versed in the Continental tradition and may well have been trained outside Ireland. Another masterpiece made later in the fifteenth century has survived – a very fine silver cross from Ballylongford, County Kerry, made on commission in 1479; it, too, belongs to the mainstream of Continental work in its style and iconography.

It is in stone that the most abundant testimony is found of craftsmanship in medieval Ireland, not only because the material is durable but because this was the field in which the Irish were most prolific. Following the Anglo-Norman conquest

LEFT *The medieval font, Dunsany church, County Meath.*

BELOW LEFT *Standing figures between the columns of the cloister, Jerpoint Abbey, County Kilkenny.*

ABOVE *Detail of the St Lawrence family tomb at Howth, County Dublin.*

we find tomb sculpture which followed Norman models from the west of England with stiff figures in high relief. Effigies of bishops in Kilfenora Cathedral, County Clare, dating from the thirteenth and fourteenth centuries, show that this tradition was followed by masons in the Gaelic west. Even after the Gaelic political and social revival in the second half of the fourteenth century most of the masons drew their inspiration from English models.

In Meath a school of stonemasons flourished from about 1450, principally under the patronage of the Plunket family who built churches on their lands at Dunsany, Killeen and Rathmore. The effigies of the deceased, sculpted in medium-high relief, lie on the mensa of their sarcophagus; on its sides in panels or niches are sculpted scenes of the Passion, figures of saints, angels and heraldic achievements. Similar work can be seen elsewhere in the Pale, notably at Howth on a free-standing chest tomb which has effigies of both the Lord St Lawrence and his wife on the mensa. Meath churches also had some handsomely sculpted baptismal fonts, probably the work of the same craftsmen who may also have carved the armorial shield of Richard, Duke of York, on the tower of Trim parish church. It must date from his residence at Trim in 1449–50. Elaborate fonts may be seen; at Clonard, where the sculpted decoration includes the Flight into Egypt, the Baptism of Christ, and shield-bearing angels; at Curraha, where the font brought from Crickstown is sculpted with a Crucifixion and Annunciation scenes and figures of the Apostles, two to a panel; at Dunsany, where the Apostles are also shown two to a panel in ogee-headed niches; and at Johnstown, where there is a rare 12-sided font from Kilcarne with the figure of an Apostle on each of its sides. The churches for which these fonts were made also had ornately carved sedilias, piscinas and traceried windows.

A school of stone sculptors from Callan have left examples of their talented work in County Kilkenny. Although mainly English in inspiration, here, outside the Pale, the influence of Celtic Christian manuscript illustration can be detected. The mason who sculpted the squat figures in ogee-headed niches on the sides of tombs in Jerpoint Abbey must have seen illuminated manuscripts six or seven centuries old which influenced his stylized treatment of the hair, beards and drapery. The cloister at Jerpoint, rebuilt in the fifteenth century, appears also to be the work of masons of the Callan school; the standing figures between the columns of the cloister recall the contemporary tomb effigies. Rory O'Tunney, a member of a family of stone sculptors working in the Callan school tradition, signed the handsome tomb of Piers Fitz Oge Butler in Kilcooly Abbey, County Tipperary. Kilcooly also has two elaborately carved sedilias, an east window in which an attempt was made to emulate flamboyant Gothic tracery, and interesting wall carvings which include a scene of the Crucifixion, two fish regarding a mermaid with a looking-glass, and St Christopher. Several places under Butler patronage in Ormond contain very superior stone carving: on the magnificent tombs in Kilkenny Cathedral, for example, in St Mary's, Callan, in Cashel Cathedral and at Gowran, but nowhere better than at Holy Cross Abbey, once a great place of pilgrimage. A relic of the True Cross which was preserved there may have been kept in an elegant rib-vaulted shrine with twisted columns, known as 'the monks' waking place'. This shrine, the ornamental three-niche sedilia in the chancel and other fifteenth-century carving reflect not only the sculptors' skill but also the cosmopolitan taste of the sixth Earl of Ormond who travelled extensively in England, on the Continent and as far as Jerusalem.

Cadaver tombs, in which the effigy of the deceased is depicted as a skeleton or a decaying corpse, were seemingly designed to remind the onlookers of mortality. One such mensa stands in the churchyard of St Peter's, Drogheda, County Louth; it shows a man and wife as skeletons in shrouds. There is another at Beaulieu in the same county. Such a macabre monument was also made for a prominent fifteenth-century Waterford merchant, who was several times mayor of his native city and added a chapel to its cathedral. He is shown lying on the mensa as a decaying corpse with slimy reptiles; around the sides of the free-standing sarcophagus the Apostles are sculpted in niches as 'weepers'.

Some sculpture flourished in the Gaelic territories in the fifteenth century, but there too the able craftsmen followed English and Continental fashions. The earliest ornamental tomb in the Irish territories appears to be that of a chief of the O'Cahans who died in 1385. The crudely stiff effigy of this Ulster ruler lies full length on the mensa of his tomb in the chancel of Dungiven Priory, County Derry, but there the 'weepers' in six trefoil-arched niches on the side are not the Apostles or saints but the chief's galloglass warriors; the canopy in the niche over the tomb is of curvilinear tracery.

County Galway boasts superb examples of virtuoso medieval stone-carving. The door of Clontuskert Abbey, which bears the date 1471, is boldly carved with a sword-bearing St Michael the Archangel with scales for weighing souls, and other figures including a mermaid and a pelican (a favourite medieval personification of charity), zoomorphic decoration, and Gothic decorative ornament such as pinnacles and crockets. In Kilconnell Friary are two well-executed tombs set in niches, one with a canopy of geometrical tracery, the other with figures of saints in six ogee-headed niches and a canopy of tracery in the flamboyant style. Laughing and smiling angels on this tomb contrast with the morbid cadaver monuments.

The canopy of a tomb-niche in Strade Friary, County Mayo, is most beautifully carved in the flamboyant Gothic style, the most accomplished tracery work in Ireland. The slab at the front of this tomb is divided into eight ogee-headed niches crowned with crocketing and each containing a figure.

Tomb-niche at Strade, County Mayo.

Acculturation The stone sculpture and the architecture of the three centuries following the Anglo-Norman invasion provide an idea of the enormous impact which the alien culture made and the influence it maintained in Ireland, even outside the limited area of English authority. The Irish, as frequently before, assimilated the aliens, but in the process they were drawn into the mainstream of western European culture in the visual arts. Gaelic Ireland clung to its language, laws and customs, but in the visual arts it adopted and copied models from abroad. In addition, despite the racial laws, intermarriage and intercourse were frequent. By 1500 most if not all of the settler community, including those in the Pale, had some Irish ancestors, while many of the Irish inhabitants could count Normans, Welsh and English among their progenitors, along with Celts and the more ancient pre-Celtic stock; some too had ancestors from the Norsemen or the galloglass mercenaries, each of which had brought their own physical characteristics.

The political events of the next century were to reduce Gaelic Ireland further and bring more foreign settlers and far more radical cultural changes. Meanwhile, the two nations, Gaelic Irish and Old English, continued to live side by side uneasily, the friction between them occasionally flaring into conflict.

By the Commissioners appointed for Stateing the Arreares of the Souldiery And of Publique Faith Debts in Ireland

Upon Composition and Agreement made with *Mrs Ester Hunt Administratrix to her late Husband Capt Thomas Hunt Deceased in behalfe of her selfe And for those of Henry Thomas Benjamin Anne Hester and Sarah Hunt Children of the said Defunct* for *all the said Defuncts* — Arrears for Service in *Ireland* from the *Last Days of December 1646 to the 5th Day of June 1649 As Capt of a Troope of Horse in Coll Chudley Cootes Regiment*

£ 16 8
714. 17. 06

There remains due from the Common-wealth to the *said Ester Hunt and the said Children of the defunct their* Executors, Administrators, or Assign's, the Sum of *Seaven hundred and ffowerteene Pounds Seaventeene Shillings and Six pence* — which is to be satisfied to the said *Ester Hunt and the said Children of the Defunct their* Executors, Administrators, or Assign's, out of the Rebels Lands, Houses, Tenements and Hereditaments in *Ireland*; or other Lands, Houses, Tenements and Hereditaments there, in the dispose of the *Common-wealth* of ENGLAND. Signed and Sealed at DUBLIN the *Six and twentieth* day of *May* 1658

Examined and entred

Tho Herbert
Dep Register

Edw Roberts
Robert Gorges
Robt Jeffreys

4 Change and Chaos

King Henry VIII

The Lordship of Ireland ended officially on 18 June 1541 with an act of parliament which declared 'That the King's highness, his heirs and successors, Kings of England, be always kings of this land of Ireland.' Henry VIII had already severed his allegiance to the Pope under whom, since the Anglo-Norman invasion, the English king held the Lordship of Ireland. Henry, therefore, had himself declared King of Ireland. In 1554, when Henry's Roman Catholic elder daughter had succeeded him to the throne, Pope Paul IV elevated Ireland into a kingdom, granting Mary I and her Spanish husband Philip the titles of Queen and King of Ireland. The innovation was in name only, for before Henry VIII's enactment the English sovereigns had long been in fact, if not in name, the kings of Ireland. Nor did the new situation put an end to the claims to absolute local sovereignty of Irish chiefs outside the Pale, or prevent them from plotting against the crown or offering the throne of Ireland to enemies of the English monarch.

Early in his reign, in 1520, Henry had instructed his Lord Lieutenant, the Earl of Surrey, to achieve by peaceful means the overall allegiance to the crown of all the Irish. After a short time assessing the situation in Ireland Surrey reported that he deemed that comprehensive submission could only be achieved by conquest, winning over Gaelic Ireland territory by territory, and colonizing the won-over lands with loyal English natives. At the time, mainly because of the cost of a military campaign, Henry did not follow Surrey's advice; but it was to become the policy of the Tudor and Stuart monarchs and of Oliver Cromwell in achieving the effective conquest of Ireland. Plots against the crown proliferated in Ireland with consequent insurrections, sometimes mounted by the Irish, sometimes in collaboration with France, Spain, the Holy Roman Empire, or the Pope.

OPPOSITE *Debenture satisfying a Cromwellian officer's arrears of pay out of confiscated lands.*

The break with Rome

Henry VIII's breach with Rome resulted in the Act of Supremacy of 1534 by which the English parliament ruled that the King should be 'taken, accepted and reputed the only Supreme Head in earth of the Church of England', and denied the Pope any greater jurisdiction than that of any other foreign bishop. This was followed two years later by a similar act of the Irish parliament in 1536 declaring the King to be supreme head of the Irish Church, thus formally severing the connection of the Irish Church with Rome. The English Augustinian priest who had performed the wedding ceremony of Henry VIII and Anne Boleyn, in flagrant defiance of the Pope's refusal to annul the King's first marriage, was rewarded by being appointed Archbishop of Dublin.

Anti-Irish laws

Also in 1536, parliament aimed a blow at Gaelic culture and society by enacting a law to promote 'English Order, Habit and Language'. Not only the Old English (the people of English and Anglo-Norman descent), but also the Gaelic Irish were forbidden to speak anything but English; nor were they permitted to wear their hair in the Irish fashion with glibes or long forelocks, to wear moustaches, saffron-dyed clothing, smocks or skirts very fully gathered in the Irish manner, Irish-style mantles, and clothing embroidered with gems or coloured glass. This was followed by measures to eliminate the linchpins of Gaelic-Irish social life, the senachies, rhymers, bards, harpers and gamesters, considered by the English to be an idle and seditious lot. The Brehons too were to be eliminated as incompatible with the extension of English legislation.

Dissolution of the monasteries

Although the break with Rome and the consequent ecclesiastical reorganization split the Irish irreconcilably, the crown found secular support in its suppression of the monasteries from those who were keen for a share of the spoils. The priory of Augustinian nuns at Grane, County Carlow, was suppressed in 1535 and the lands granted to Grey, the Lord Deputy, and his male heirs. The dissolution of five of the great Cistercian abbeys in Leinster soon followed; by 1537, with the suppression of Bective, Baltinglass, Graiguenamanagh (Duiske), Dunbrody and Tintern, a mortal blow had been dealt to monastic life in the province.

Ousted abbots and abbesses were usually granted a pension. Occasionally, where the new leaseholders were slow to take possession, the monastic communities managed to hang on for a while. In other places the monks contrived to remain in the vicinity of their former buildings on the pretext of serving the local population. Invariably in the first distributions monastic lands went to loyal servants of the crown. Of the five Cistercian foundations mentioned Bective went first in 1537 to Thomas Agard, an assistant to the Vice-Treasurer; seven years later it was held by John Alen, the Lord Chancellor, and in 1552 the lease was sold for £1,380 to Andrew Wyse, the Vice-Treasurer. The site of Baltinglass Abbey was granted first in 1541 by patent to Thomas Eustace, Viscount Baltinglass, and then in 1556 with other monastic lands to Sir Edmund Butler. Graiguenamanagh went in 1538 to the Earl of Ormond. Most of Dunbrody was granted in 1545 to Sir Osbert Itchingham, Marshal of the Army. Tintern went to John Brereton, a son of the Lord Chancellor and Lord Justice Sir William Brereton who had also acted as Lord Deputy in 1540.

All over Leinster, where the monasteries were most speedily suppressed, there were men eager for pickings. Two important Augustinian foundations, St Wolstan's in County Kildare and Duleek in County Louth, went in 1536 and 1538 respectively to John Alen, then Master of the Rolls, and Edward Beck, a Bristol merchant. The great Benedictine Abbey at Fore in County Westmeath was acquired in 1540 by an Englishman, Matthew King, Clerk of the Check. Thomas Casey, a merchant of Athboy, County Meath, and judging by his name presumably of Irish origin, purchased the Carmelite friary in his home town in 1542; he converted the church into a mill and a convent building into a mansion, using stones from the cloister to repair it. The Franciscan friary in O'More country at Stradbally, County Leix, did not fall into English hands until the 1560s. It was granted to an English soldier, Francis Cosby, General of the Lord Deputy's kern, who had earlier acquired lands of the nunnery of Hogges, Dublin, in 1537. It is interesting that the direct descendant in the male line in the eleventh generation of this Francis Cosby, Major Errold A.S.Cosby, is still the owner of part of the lands and lives at Stradbally Hall, on the site of the friary acquired by his ancestor.

After the Pale and the earldom of Ormonde, the suppression was extended to the isolated territories of the crown, to the earldom of Desmond, held nominally as a feudal fief of the crown but whose ruler refused to acknowledge the King's jurisdiction, to Thomond, and, in a more haphazard fashion, to the sovereign territories of the Gaelic rulers in Connacht and Ulster. The campaign failed to make an effective impact there in Henry VIII's reign, and it was not until Elizabeth's time that a general suppression was achieved. Many of the monasteries underwent a series of vicissitudes. At Sligo, where Queen Elizabeth allowed the Dominicans to stay at the request of the O'Conor Sligo because she was told that they were living as secular priests, the friars have maintained an uninterrupted presence until the present day. At Donegal, where their friary was destroyed, the Franciscans remained in the district, and the monks who compiled the *Annals of The Four Masters* lived there. At Moyne in County Mayo an English widow held the Franciscan friary and its lands in 1606, and rented the church and a few cells to the friars. However, in places where mendicant friars persisted, with the connivance of a charitable landlord or of the people, their existence was precarious. Even landowners sympathetic to the monks acquired confiscated monastic properties, such as the Brownes who became Earls of Kenmare, and the Burkes, Earls of Clanrickarde.

Changes in land tenure and inheritance

As part of the policy of consolidation the Irish chiefs were urged to surrender their lands to the crown, which would immediately re-grant them under the royal seal as hereditary estates held under the crown. The clansmen were not pleased with this change in the system of tenure whereby their own ancient rights were extinguished and the clan lands became the personal estate of the chief, to pass on his death to his male heirs according to the English system of primogeniture.

In an effort to integrate some of the Gaelic magnates into the English system of nobility and procure their loyalty, the King bestowed hereditary peerages on men who already considered themselves to be sovereign princes, such as Morrogh O'Brien who was created Earl of Thomond, and Conn Bacach O'Neill, the most powerful man in Ulster, who had prostrated himself before the King of England and was created Earl of Tyrone. According to the ancient Irish practice of tanistry, at Conn's death the O'Neill overlordship of Ulster would not have passed automatically to his eldest son, or even to any of his sons, but to a successful candidate from within the extended family group. However, the patent of the earldom required that he be succeeded in that honour by his eldest son, according to English practice. Conn's family arrangements, however, followed the Gaelic life-style: he was married to at least three wives, and he had at least six children who had some claim to be considered legitimate; but Conn nominated one of his several illegitimate sons as his eldest son and successor. The conflict which ensued between Shane O'Neill, who claimed to be Conn's eldest legitimate son and was, in any case, the tanist, and Matthew, the bastard son, who was made the heir to the earldom when it was granted, was a direct outcome of the conflict between the English and Irish institutional systems. Not without difficulty, and only through military intervention, was the English system finally imposed in all Ireland.

Tudor conquest and colonization

Under Edward VI, the son and successor of Henry VIII, the Pale was enlarged by a military thrust into Offaly and Leix, where forts were constructed to help hold the territories taken from the O'Connor Faly and O'More chiefs. Under Mary I, the next monarch and a Roman Catholic, the colonization of these lands was implemented, following Surrey's earlier advice to Henry VIII. The names of Maryborough (now Portlaoise, County Leix) and Philipstown (now Daingean, County Offaly) long stood as a reminder of the plantation of those counties in the reign of Mary Tudor and her Spanish husband; the newly shired territories, now Leix and Offaly, became the Queen's County and the King's County. The lands were leased to loyal English subjects, mostly new settlers, and the Irish who did not collaborate had to move farther west, from where they did their best to harass the new inhabitants.

Shane O'Neill, who in 1566 asked the French to help him expel the English, was defeated in 1567. His pickled head was sent to Dublin and impaled on a spike in the castle wall to remind all who saw it that Elizabeth was Queen and determined to extend her writ to embrace all Ireland. The time was ripe to promote a colonial plantation in Ulster. The authorities, anxious to cut the cost of the campaign to subdue Ireland, were happy to allow private entrepreneurs to establish programmes of settlement.

Sir Thomas Smith, a classics scholar in the best Renaissance tradition, obtained an extensive grant of the lands of the O'Neills of Clandeboy in the south-east of the present province of Ulster, including the Ards peninsula. Smith saw himself as an ancient Roman administrator, bringing the light of civilization to a barbarian land. Settlers arrived in 1572. The plan was to expel all the Irish but the labourers, and to put these to work under the new English farmers. The enterprise collapsed for want of military protection to protect the settlers from the Irish.

The same spirit which prompted the English to establish colonies in America moved them to attempt colonial enterprises in Ireland, whose native inhabitants they

DRAVN AFTER · THE · QVICKE

Contemporary drawing of Irish kerne.

regarded with the same disdain as the North American Indians and Caribs, and whom they eliminated with comparable brutality.

Walter Devereux, Earl of Essex, received from Queen Elizabeth I a vast grant of land in Ulster and a large loan to finance a colonial venture. It too was a failure, although Essex might have been more successful if he had received adequate financial backing from London, but again the authorities baulked at military expenditure. Essex's gratuitous massacre of 200 O'Neill followers at Belfast in 1574, and the brutal massacre of several hundred people – including the women and children of the MacDonnels on Rathlin Island, in which Francis Drake took part in 1575 – increased Irish resentment. They increased their efforts to engage foreign help to oust the English.

Pope Gregory XIII gave his backing to a papal expeditionary force in 1578 but the 600 men who landed in County Kerry in 1580 with ammunition to start the war were all slaughtered by the English. The Earl of Desmond, in open rebellion against the Queen, tried desperately to get further help from Spain, but without success. The Pope released the Irish from allegiance to Elizabeth and granted a plenary indulgence to all who took up arms against the sovereign who in the eyes of Rome was illegitimate and a heretic.

The Irish, however, poorly organized and lacking co-ordination, needed more substantial assistance. It was not forthcoming. The Desmond risings were suppressed, the power of the great earls was broken, and the vast, rich palatinate, which for centuries they had ruled virtually as sovereigns, was seized. A plantation of English adventurers and settlers on the confiscated Desmond lands in Munster soon followed.

English adventurers received lots of 4,000, 6,000, 8,000 and 12,000 acres on which they settled tenants, who in turn brought over sub-tenants. Altogether over half a million acres were redistributed. Land-hungry sons of the gentry, yeoman farmers and husbandmen came over from England, bringing with them farming equipment and tools currently in use there. Among these English was the poet Edmund Spenser, who had served in Ireland as secretary to the Lord Deputy and had been present when the papal force was butchered in Kerry. Spenser obtained an estate in County Cork, but had to flee when rebels burned his tower-house residence, Kilcolman Castle, in 1598. Because many settlers returned to England, frightened and discouraged by the animosity of the dispossessed Irish, the Elizabethan plantation of Munster is often thought of as a failure. It did, however, have a continuity; the names of Elizabethan settlers such as Daunt, Beamish, Blennerhasset and Spring still survive there today.

The most energetic and successful of the Elizabethans in Ireland was Richard Boyle, created Earl of Cork in 1620. Undiscouraged after early reverses, Boyle acquired thousands of acres of fertile land in Munster at a bargain price from Sir Walter Ralegh, to whom the estates had been granted but who was glad to dispose of them. With prodigious foresight and regardless of expense, Boyle initiated a programme of improvement. He built bridges, founded and laid out towns, constructed harbours and built castles. He brought skilled settlers from England to introduce manufacture and mechanical arts, one of his major enterprises being the establishment of a highly profitable ironworks; he also promoted the woollen and linen industries, timber processing and fisheries.

Boyle's immigrant workers were not the only ones to contribute technology. Sir Henry Sidney brought Flemish weavers and tanners to Swords, County Dublin, in the 1570s; in the next century the Irish economy benefited from the arrival of Dutch textile workers and of Huguenot refugees from France, among whom were silversmiths, goldsmiths, watchmakers and clockmakers, silk-weavers and other skilled artisans. The growth of urban communities attracted tradesmen from England – bakers, butchers, brewers, chandlers, cutlers, tailors, coopers, wig-makers, apothecaries, shoemakers, printers and booksellers, hatters, glovers and tobacconists. Flemish artists were painting portraits in Ireland in the sixteenth century, and in the seventeenth century painters from England and the Continent came to work there, as did English actors and playwrights.

As the Elizabethan programme of colonization and subjugation progressed, the Hibernicized families of Anglo-Norman origin and the Irish princes were brought to order in Connacht. In the 1590s commissioners were dispatched to the province to assess the land, fix rents and establish the crown's dues. Recalcitrant rulers like Brian O'Rorke of Breffni, who harboured survivors of the Spanish Armada, were executed and their territories forfeited.

The failure of the last Irish rebellion of Elizabeth's reign paved the way for the colonization of Ulster. In 1595 Hugh O'Neill, Earl of Tyrone and grandson of Conn, the first Earl, agreed to lead a rebel confederacy against the crown. His training in England, where he had the chance to study military tactics, was useful in rebellion against his mentors. At first successful, the rising ended in failure. Spanish help, on which O'Neill was counting, arrived too late; the English had had enough time to organize an efficient resistance. The Spanish force of nearly 5,000 men landed on the south coast at Kinsale, County Cork. This meant that O'Neill and his northern allies had to march their men across the length of Ireland from north to south to join the Spaniards. Had the Irish risen as a man along O'Neill's route, the English might have been trounced. As it was, the Irish were far from united. Moreover, an Irishman, Brian Oge Mac Mahon – a traitor in the eyes of the Irish, a loyal subject in the eyes of the English – forewarned the English of the battle strategy of his own countrymen at Kinsale; the Irish-Spanish force was defeated in 1601 by the disciplined, well-organized troops of the English commander, Mountjoy.

A few years later, in autumn 1607, Hugh O'Neill, Earl of Tyrone, and Rory O'Donnell, Earl of Tyrconnell and the Maguire, the former ruler of Fermanagh, embarked at Rathmullan, County Donegal, for the Continent with a number of followers. Their departure, remembered as the Flight of the Earls, was dictated by their preference for exile to a life of undignified submission. Their going was lamented by the poets and people of Ulster. 'Now stolen is the soul from Eire's breast', deplored the O'Donnell bard in his commemorative ode. For the architects of English colonialism, however, the departure of the Earls paved the way for the smoother parcelling out and resettlement of their forfeited estates.

The Plantation of Ulster

The Plantation of Ulster was the most impressive, and, in its encouragement of immigration, the most important of the colonial programmes. Its far-reaching consequences still trouble Ireland today. In the six escheated Ulster counties, the ancient *termon* and *erenagh* lands were almost all assigned to the Protestant bishops, the spiritual lords of the Established Church. In County Londonderry, formed in 1613 from Derry with the former county of Coleraine and most of the barony of Loughinsholin in Tyrone, these ecclesiastical estates amounted to almost one quarter of all the available land. Lands were also assigned to the newly incorporated towns and to a free school in each county; Trinity College, Dublin, received nearly 100,000 acres of Ulster. By a special agreement, over half the land in County Londonderry went to the City of London. Some large individual grants went to Englishmen such as Sir Thomas Phillips who got four per cent of County Londonderry, and the Lord Deputy, Sir Arthur Chichester, who got all of the barony of Inishowen that was not church land. The native Irish were not entirely excluded, and received, for example, 10 per cent of County Londonderry. A few Irish nobles benefited, such as Sir Tirlogh Mac Henry O'Neill, who received the southern half of the barony of Fews, Brian Crossagh O'Neill and Conor Roe Maguire in east Fermanagh, Mulmory Og O'Reilly in County Cavan, and Tirlogh O'Boyle in County Donegal.

The principle of the plantation scheme in Ulster was to clear given areas of Irish inhabitants and resettle them with English or Scottish tenants brought over by entrepreneurs, called 'undertakers'. The Irish were restricted to reside on lands granted to Irish collaborators considered loyal to the crown, church lands, and lands granted to former English army officers, known as servitors. The allotments of land came in three sizes and with various obligations to the grantees, such as to bring over a stipulated quota of tenants from England or Scotland, and to build houses and defences. The Irish who were fortunate enough to get an allocation had to pay double rent and use only English methods of tillage and husbandry. The conditions of the scheme required the undertakers to take up residence in Ireland by autumn 1610, and to fulfil their obligations regarding building and bringing over settlers by Easter 1613. The removal of the Irish was not easy. In 1618 fines were levied in an effort to enforce the segregation, but in 1628 the government had to amend their ban and allow Irish tenants to live on one quarter of the English and Scottish estates on payment of fines and double rents.

With minor variations the policy of resettlement was extended to Leitrim and Longford and the unsettled parts of Leix and Offaly, and to part of County Wexford. The counties of Antrim and Down, which were resettled privately, received the highest proportion of immigrants. By 1622 about 7,500 British were residing in Down and Antrim, while the six escheated counties of Ulster, Londonderry, Donegal, Tyrone, Fermanagh, Cavan and Armagh contained about 3,700 settler families, almost equally divided between Scots and English.

The new landowners brought over artisans as well as farmers. Sir James Hamilton, for example, who imported building materials from England and Scotland for his improvements in County Down, also brought over 20 workers who were making bricks and stone and timber artefacts for his buildings in 1611.

Twenty-three urban communities were laid out on a grid plan in Ulster with their public buildings on a central square or diamond. Before the plantation, Carrickfergus and Newry were the only urban nuclei of any consequence in the province.

The new architecture

A unique survivor of Tudor English fashion, which reached the Pale and the Anglophile aristocracy in the sixteenth century, is the manor house built by 'Black Tom' Butler, tenth Earl of Ormonde, adjacent to his medieval castle at Carrick-on-Suir, County Tipperary, at a time when the nobles were still living in uncomfortable towers. The Earl, brought up at the English court, was a favourite of Queen Elizabeth to whom he was related through her mother's family, the Boleyns. He may, in fact, have been the Queen's lover; her attentions to him while at her court in England from 1565 to 1569 were a cause for scandal. Although this Earl of Ormonde avowed strong Irish sympathies he professed unswerving loyalty to the crown and was a staunch supporter of law and order. Considering his early upbringing in England, his time at court in the 1560s and his later sojourns there in 1572 and 1579, it is not surprising that in the 1560s he built an Irish residence in the gracious style of the non-fortified manors he had seen. Of stone and brick with brick gables and chimneys, numerous mullioned windows and a splendid galleried hall with a stuccoed ceiling and two chimney-pieces, the house was planned with extensive offices and the creature comfort of several privies.

In the Pale and the provincial cities, cage-work houses were built in the style of those common in Tudor England. These quaint timber buildings with exposed oak beams and overhanging upper storeys have all now vanished, but until the early eighteenth century they were common in Dublin, Limerick, Cork and Drogheda; the last of them were demolished only in the nineteenth century. An early drawing of one of the houses at Drogheda shows what they were like.

By the end of the sixteenth century gabled, stone-built houses were appearing in Irish towns. They can be seen in early townscape paintings, and a few of them survive. There is a row of these houses in the main street of Youghal, a town which also has a gabled mansion dating from the late sixteenth century which may have been the residence of Sir Walter Ralegh. Like the Earl of Ormonde's manor house, it is very English in appearance.

Outside the towns, adventurers who wanted a residence on their estates built stout, defensible castles. The surviving shell of the castle at Mallow, built at the end of the sixteenth century by Sir Thomas Norreys, gives us an idea of an important late Elizabethan residence in Ireland. At the time it was described as a 'goodly fair and sumptuous house'. Most of the settlers, however, lived in tower-houses. Frequently they built dwelling houses on to and communicating with a medieval castle.

Scottish settlers in Ulster built in the style of their native country. Examples with distinctive pepperpot turrets survive at Ballygalley, County Antrim, where the castle

Carrick-on-Suir Castle, County Tipperary.

was built by a settler from Greenock in 1625; at Monea, County Fermanagh, where the chambers are set diagonally on the towers, with their projecting corners supported by strongly moulded courses of corbels (like the castle at Claypotts, near Dundee); and at Castle Balfour, also in County Fermanagh.

There was considerable building activity in Ireland, more in fact than is now apparent; many of the houses were modest and unpretentious and few survive. Among the most important were Joymount, the great turreted mansion of Sir Arthur Chichester at Carrickfergus, County Antrim, built about 1610, Sir Toby Caulfield's impressive mansion at Charlemont, County Tyrone, built between 1622 and 1624 (both of these have been demolished), Sir Basil Brooke's gabled mansion adjoining the medieval castle at Donegal, built in the 1620s and now in ruins, and Archbishop Loftus's Rathfarnham Castle, County Dublin, built in 1585, which has been altered and is still inhabited. Coppinger's Court, built by Sir Walter Coppinger about 1616, with two towers at the front and one at the back, is a ruin. Court Devenish, a fine, stone-built town mansion, was built at Athlone about 1620.

Kanturk Castle, County Cork, which resembles Rathfarnham in its plan, is of interest because it was built by a Gaelic chief, Dermot MacOwen MacDonogh MacCarthy of Duhallow. The authorities were perturbed at the size of such a castle

in the hands of an Irish chief, so although he professed loyalty to the crown he was prevented from finishing it. The shell of the great four-storey building flanked by five-storey towers still stands; it was never roofed. Its most attractive feature is a handsome doorway which shows that Renaissance style was gradually filtering into Ireland.

Tomb sculpture of the early seventeenth century also occasionally reveals classical Renaissance influence, as, for example, on the sarcophagus of Nicholas White, 1622, formerly at Clonmel and now at St Patrick's Well, County Tipperary.

The first purpose-built Protestant church in Ireland was erected at Newry, County Down, in 1579. Like most of the few churches built in the reigns of Elizabeth I, James I and Charles I, its original form has been disguised by subsequent rebuilding and additions. It was unnecessary for the Established Church to erect new parish churches or cathedrals, for in most places they appropriated the pre-Reformation churches and cathedrals of the old faith. The flurry of Protestant church-building was to come much later. Protestant churches were, however, required to serve the settlers in the new urban developments. At Bandon, County Cork, Richard Boyle, later first Earl of Cork, built Kilbrogan parish church for his settlers in 1610. In 1628 the City of London Corporation financed the construction of a cathedral to

ABOVE *Ballinderry Middle Church, County Antrim, is a rare and well-preserved example of a seventeenth-century Protestant settlers' church.*

RIGHT *Cagework house, Drogheda, County Louth, from a drawing made before 1825.*

ABOVE *House at Kilkenny built by a family of prosperous merchants named Rothe.*

LEFT *Sixteenth-century stone-built house in Main Street, Youghal, County Cork.*

replace the ancient cathedral of St Columcille at Derry which had been destroyed in the rebellion. The new cathedral, for the burgeoning immigrant population attracted by the colonial enterprise of the London companies, was built in the late Gothic style of the London City churches of the late Middle Ages.

A French traveller who visited Ireland in 1644 remarked that the residences of the nobility were high rectangular towers with thatched roofs and no more light than what came in through narrow slits. He found these tower-houses barely furnished and noted that at night the inhabitants slept on beds of rushes strewn on the floor. This description must have fitted the dwellings of the less affluent settler landlords in rural areas and most of the Gaelic nobles, but in the towns affluent merchants like the Rothes of Kilkenny lived in substantial stone houses with plenty of windows. The Rothe house in Kilkenny, which can be visited, was built in 1594 and additions were made on its courtyards at the rear over the next 20 years. In rural areas too there were a number of large houses built by the wealthier proprietors in the reign of Charles I until the Irish Insurrection of 1641, and the disturbances of the Civil War put a halt to almost all building activity.

The Carolean houses, half-house, half-castle, are best described as strong-houses, their defensible character usually being evident in their plan as well as in such fortifications as machicolations and firing holes. They did, however, concede to fashion in having large, well-lit apartments. Many-gabled Burncourt in County Tipperary, built by Sir Richard Everard in 1641, has four protecting towers at the angles of the house, linked by a timber guard-walk carried on corbels. Flanking towers at the four corners was a popular plan, followed, for example, at Mount Long, built in 1631, and Monkstown, built in 1636, both in County Cork and both with a four-storey tower at each corner of a three-storey block. Leamaneh, County Clare, built about 1640 by Conor O'Brien, is a rarer example of a strong-house built by a Gaelic nobleman. Here the mansion was joined to an earlier tower at one end. Daniel O'Madden's Derryhivenny, County Galway, built shortly after Leamaneh, is still in the tower-house tradition.

Probably the most elegant house built in the reign of Charles I was Jigginstown, County Kildare, an ambitious red-brick mansion with a 380-ft frontage built by the Lord Deputy, the Earl of Strafford. When Strafford was enquiring into land tenure in Connacht he requisitioned a new mansion which rivalled his own. This was Portumna Castle, County Galway, built by the rich fourth Earl of Clanrickarde who lived mostly in England. Being in trouble-prone Connacht, Portumna was planned as a strong-house following the arrangement of four towers flanking the rectangular central block, consisting in this case of four bays on three storeys and attics over a basement. The crenellated parapet has delightful curvilinear gables ornamented with balls on finials. The house, which has a fine Renaissance door-case, is approached through a series of axial gateways and courtyards. The houses of prosperous Galway merchants also had fine Renaissance doorways.

If most of the tower-houses were sparsely furnished and lacking in comforts, this was not true of all the mansions of Charles I's reign. The claims of householders who lost their property in the Irish Insurrection of 1641 include inventories listing hangings, tapestries, richly embroidered cushions, Venetian glass, feather beds, clocks and couches. The houses of town merchants were well furnished with bedsteads, chests, presses, tables, stools, cushions and carpets as well as household objects in brass, pewter and silver.

The 1641 rising

The seething discontent among the Ulster nobles who instigated an insurrection in 1641 was caused by their inability to adapt to the new social and economic conditions created by the resettlement of their province. This discontent was certainly aggravated by the religious issue. The official measures against Catholicism, by which the crown hoped to strengthen loyal Protestant control of Ireland, gave cause for real grievance. Discriminatory legislation introduced under James I included the banishment of clergy and the levying of fines for recusancy. The prevailing English belief was that Roman Catholics were bound to be disloyal because the Pope's claim to approve or depose a ruler prevented them from giving both spiritual allegiance to the pontiff and temporal allegiance to the monarch. This indeed was the quandary in which those Roman Catholics in Ireland who would have been loyal to the crown, such as many of the Old English, found themselves.

The leader of the conspiracy was Rory O'More, whose family had been chiefs in the midlands but who was living on his estate in County Armagh. His earliest fellow conspirators were Conor, Lord Maguire and Sir Phelim O'Neill. As has so often happened in Irish history, an Irishman betrayed the plans of his countrymen. The rebels' attack on Dublin Castle in autumn 1641, by means of which they aimed to paralyse the administration, was foiled by the government who had been forewarned by Owen O'Connolly, foster-brother of one of the leaders of the rising, Hugh Oge Mac Mahon. The simultaneous insurrection in Ulster, however, was successful and within a short time the rebels moved southwards, took Dundalk, and besieged Drogheda. In the summer of 1642 Owen Roe O'Neill, who had been serving in the Spanish army in Flanders, landed in County Donegal with men and arms for the revolt, which spread to all Ireland.

It had not been the intention of the leaders of the rebellion to provoke a mass slaughter of settlers, but the undisciplined and angry rebels waited neither for orders nor sanctions in setting savagely upon the New English. Several thousand settlers perished; some were massacred by the violent, exasperated Irish, and some died of sickness and starvation after being ejected from their homes. Exaggerated reports of the sufferings of the settlers incited a brutal backlash in which many Roman Catholics lost their lives in retaliatory massacres.

The Civil War

For all parties in Ireland – Gaelic nobles, almost overwhelmingly Roman Catholic, Old English nobles, divided, but mostly Roman Catholic, New English, almost all Protestant, and all still reeling from the effects of the rebellion – the political strife in England between King and parliament further complicated the issue of allegiance. In England there was a clear-cut division between royalists and parliamentarians. In Ireland there were Roman Catholics of Old English origin and a few of Gaelic origin who were willing to support the monarch against what they saw as a worse enemy. The bulk of the Gaelic or Old Irish were unwilling to ally themselves with a heretic monarch, even in the face of a more dangerous power. The majority of the New English were sympathetic to the puritan ethic and the principles of the parliamentarians who opposed the King, but among the Protestant settler community there were also royalists. Not a few changed sides in mid-conflict, adding to the uncertainty and chaos which reigned in Ireland. The arrival in 1645 of the papal nuncio, Cardinal Rinuccini, with a mandate to restore and re-establish the public exercise of the Roman Catholic faith in Ireland, did not unite the Catholic factions as intended, but ended by exacerbating their differences.

The Cromwellian conquest

If all the Roman Catholics in Ireland had united and if, moreover, Catholic and Protestant royalists had not been divided, they might have maintained the country for the royalists and used their bargaining power to press for the establishment of a regime with equitable laws. Weakened by their divisions, however, they were utterly crushed. In August 1649 Cromwell landed at Ringsend with 8,000 infantry and 4,000 cavalry to relieve the parliamentarian forces holding Dublin and to accomplish the conquest of Ireland, which he did speedily and ruthlessly. The King had been executed a few months earlier and it was essential to Cromwell's

A tower on the breached walls of Clonmel, County Tipperary.

policy to secure Ireland and prevent it from becoming a royalist state in opposition to the Commonwealth established in England.

First taking Drogheda, where he ordered the slaughter of almost the entire garrison and the transportation to Barbados of the few survivors, Cromwell detached a force to march northwards, where they took Carrickfergus. Cromwell himself took the main body of the army southwards. At Wexford about 2,000 townspeople were slaughtered indiscriminately. The opposition was unable to remedy its lack of unity and Cromwell drove on, pushing his conquest inland. Kilkenny surrendered in March 1650; in May Cromwell marched into Clonmel, where he lost 2,000 men in overcoming the defending garrison. Carlow fell to the parliamentarians in July, Waterford in August; Limerick surrendered in October, and Galway, the last remaining fortified town, in April 1652. One by one the opposing bands laid down their arms; the last formal surrender took place in County Cavan in April 1653. In their four-year campaign the parliamentarians had reduced all the opposition, but had also reduced the country to a state of hunger, disease and misery, and left such a trail of carnage that the hatred and fear which it engendered lasted for centuries.

Social upheaval

Draconian measures were taken against Roman Catholics. Hundreds were executed after peremptory trials and several thousand Irish were forcibly transported to the West Indies and Virginia. After the Civil War there were about 8,000 Irish in Barbados alone; in Montserrat there were 2,000, and a sizeable number in Jamaica too. A comprehensive programme of land confiscation was initiated which resulted in major social upheaval. Cromwell arranged to settle the arrears of pay to his army by granting them confiscated land. Forfeiting landowners were transplanted with their families to rural Connacht and parts of County Clare. The English adventurers claimed over one million acres of profitable land. In the Cromwellian plantation scheme adventurers and ex-soldiers were mixed, for the greater security of the settlement. Adventurers with large claims were allotted estates of several thousand acres, but there were small claimants too who drew lots of less than 100. Over 30,000 debentures were issued to soldiers, about two-thirds of whom sold them and about one-third took possession of land to the value of their debentures. Although the Cromwellian government was not prepared to extend any toleration to Roman

Catholics, there were few conversions. In the vast redistribution of land many of the Old English suffered along with the Gaelic Irish, and many former landowners became tenants of the new proprietors.

The Restoration settlements

On the return of Charles II to the throne in 1660, Irish Roman Catholics hoped for both religious toleration and recovery of their estates, but they were largely disappointed. The Protestant settlers were determined to keep their estates, and no satisfactory solution could be found to content both them and those Roman Catholics who had been continually loyal to the King, some of whom had been with him in exile in France. In the 1660 settlement all soldiers and adventurers, except those who had been refused a pardon, were allowed to keep their lands. In a few cases, where the land was returned to former owners who qualified as 'Innocent Papists', the new owners were recompensed with grants elsewhere. Grants were also made to the '49 Officers – Protestants, mostly English – who had served in the royalist forces in Ireland before June 1649.

Discontent followed. An act of 1665 requiring soldiers and adventurers to relinquish one-third of their lands so that all the claims could be satisfied (including the restoration to 54 Roman Catholics of estates of 2,000 acres), caused further discontent among the soldier-adventurer population, while the Roman Catholics on the whole felt that they still had not been fairly treated.

In 1670 the population of Ireland comprised the Gaels of pre-Celtic and Celtic stock, the Old English of Anglo-Norman, Welsh and English stock, the New English of the Tudor plantations, the New English and Scots of the plantations in the reign of James I, the New English of the Cromwellian settlement and a few immigrants from the Continent, mostly French, Flemish and Walloon refugees. Each group was aware of its identity, but in the process of change in the seventeenth century the culture of the Old English failed to survive, while that of the New English groups tended to coalesce, so that by the end of the century there were roughly two divisions – Planters and Irish.

Building and rebuilding activity

In Dublin, where the merchants and city dwellers were less concerned about any uncertainties of their possession, and where the brilliant and urbane Restoration Viceroy, the Duke of Ormonde, headed a fast-expanding administration, the 1660s and 1670s were decades of expansion and relative prosperity, influenced by the gaiety, enthusiasm and worldliness of Restoration England. Building was encouraged; many old timber buildings were replaced by stone and brick dwellings, while new residential areas were developed. The curvilinear gable and pediment made its appearance as a result of the arrival in Dublin of Protestant refugees from France and the Netherlands. Christ Church Cathedral was repaired, St Patrick's was reroofed, and new bells were installed in both cathedrals. New churches were built for Protestant worship.

The country landowners, less sure of their security of tenure and often short of cash, were slower to build or rebuild. Many continued to inhabit medieval buildings, sometimes adding a modest residence to an old tower, as did the Cromwellian settler at Castle Salem, County Cork.

Those with money to build came from an adventurer-settler-soldier background. Sir Henry Tichborne, Marshal of the Army in Ireland, or possibly his son William, built a handsome house at Beaulieu, County Louth, on the lands which were confirmed to him under the Acts of Settlement. It was one of the first Irish mansions built without fortification, a two-storey house with attic dormers in a high hipped roof in the 'Artisan' style, fashionable a few years earlier in England. At Kilkenny, where the Duke of Ormonde's example provided an impetus, the Duke himself commissioned extensive rebuilding on his castle to make it look like a French château with high-pitched roofs, and it was richly decorated with tapestries, Spanish leather hangings, statuary and paintings. Some new houses of this period had a distinctly Continental air, with wings *en échelon* like Ballintober, County Cork, Morristown Lattin, County Kildare, and Rich Hill, County Armagh, where Dutch gables mask the roof ridges. Less grand houses of the period resembled English yeoman dwellings, long and low with dormered attics and high chimneystacks. A favourite Irish plan included a single-bay return at the rear to contain the stair.

The most distinguished building of the late seventeenth century, however, is neither a residence nor a church but the Royal Hospital at Kilmainham, Dublin, built in the 1680s at the instigation of Charles II to house war veterans. The architect, Sir William Robinson, built it in the Classical style more widespread in France and the Netherlands than in England.

Painting

The Restoration heralded the real beginning of painting in Ireland. French and Dutch artists, and those influenced by the French and Dutch schools, were among the first. James Gandy, an English painter who enjoyed the Duke of Ormonde's patronage, is said to have been a pupil of Van Dyck. Gaspar Smitz, a painter who came to Ireland in the 1670s from the Netherlands via England, worked in Dublin for about 30 years until his death there. The first Irish-born painter of note, Garret Morphey, may have been trained by Smitz and visited the Netherlands, where he was influenced by other Dutch artists such as the Netschers. In his work Morphey combined Dutch and English influences. One English painter who worked in Ireland for some years, John Michael Wright, executed a number of excellent portraits.

Education

As part of the Tudor colonial programme a few parish schools were established in Ireland in the reign of Henry VIII to teach the English language. Under Elizabeth I, diocesan schools were established and a parliamentary act of 1570 provided for one in the principal shire town of each diocese under the direction of an English master. In the Ulster plantation scheme provision was made for the establishment of at least one free school in each of the six escheated counties. These were all Protestant schools designed to promote the growth of Protestantism, but a report of 1633 mentioned that some had been infiltrated by 'Popish school-masters'. Erasmus Smith, a London merchant adventurer, established free English-type grammar schools at Drogheda, Tipperary and Galway, under a royal charter of 1669 which decreed that the master should be chosen by the Protestant bishop or archbishop. Smith clearly stated that his aim was to propagate the Protestant faith. The curriculum included Writing, Arithmetic, Latin, Greek and Hebrew, and students could prepare for entrance to university.

At the instigation of Henry Ussher, the Protestant primate, Ireland's first university, Trinity College, Dublin, was founded in 1593. Among the first students was James Ussher, born in 1581 in Dublin, a future Protestant archbishop of Armagh and primate of Ireland. A brilliant student, and at an early age a learned, controversial theologian, he came to be respected by all his contemporaries of both faiths. In the course of his work *The Antiquities of British Churches*, he found and acquired the *Book of Kells*, which came to Trinity College library with his books and manuscripts in 1661.

For the first 50 years of its existence, although a Protestant establishment, Trinity College also admitted Roman Catholic students. It was the *alma mater* of most of the Protestant clergy of Ireland for more than 300 years and the university attended by the sons of the Protestant gentry, nobility and substantial merchants.

Before their disruption by the chaotic events and periods of strife in the sixteenth and seventeenth centuries, the traditional Gaelic schools in Ireland imparted a high standard of instruction in their specialized subjects. Men like Dermot O'Meara, a pathologist from Tipperary and author of a Latin medical text published at Dublin

*James Ussher (1581–1657),
Archbishop of Armagh and
Protestant primate of Ireland. He
was recognized as one of the most
learned men in Ireland even by
Roman Catholic theologians who
referred to him as 'the pseudoprimate'.*

in 1611, received his early training under the hereditary physicians in Ireland before going to Oxford, where he obtained a doctorate. Niall O'Glacan, who became physician to the King of France and Professor of Medicine at the Universities of Toulouse and Bologna, was schooled by hereditary physicians in Ireland before going abroad. Conly Cashin, the author of a Latin treatise on fevers in 1667, and Bernard Connor of Kerry who died in 1698, both highly skilled doctors, are other examples of alumni of the traditional schools. When the royal physicians in London were unable to diagnose or treat Primate Ussher for an obstinate disease he was treated and cured on his return to Ireland in 1626 by Dr Arthur, a Roman Catholic physician from Limerick. The traditional schools of the poets, too, could boast such alumni as Father Hugh MacCaghwell OFM (alias Hugo Cavellus), Tadhg Dall O'hUigginn who died in 1591, Eochaidh O'Hussey, the bard of the Maguires who died in 1612, and Fearghal Og Mac Ward, the bard of the O'Donnells, who composed a poignant lament on the Flight of the Earls.

Organized persecution and legislation hampered and eventually extinguished most Roman Catholic schools such as those established by the Jesuits in the sixteenth century. The school founded by Dominic Lynch at Galway and the school of Peter White at Waterford, which had a high reputation for classical teaching, both managed to flourish under James I. But oppression and restrictions increasingly made the Roman Catholic Irish turn to foreign schools for higher education. The restrictions forced aspirants to the Roman Catholic priesthood in particular to seek training on the Continent; as a result the rift between the Catholics and Protestants was widened in Ireland because their Continental education drew the Irish clergy closer to Rome and to Roman Catholic Europe. Irish colleges were founded in several European countries for the education of seminarians, among them the college at Salamanca in 1592 and at Lisbon the following year. Of the seventeenth-century Irish colleges the most notable were in Paris, founded in 1605, in Rome, founded in 1625, and at Louvain in what is now Belgium, founded in 1606.

James II (LEFT) *and*
William III (RIGHT).

The war of the two kings

On the death of Charles II in 1685 his Roman Catholic brother succeeded him as James II. In 1687 the new king appointed as his Irish Viceroy a staunch Roman Catholic, Richard Talbot, created Earl of Tyrconnell. In 1688, in the face of strong anti-Catholic sentiment in England, the King fled to France. The throne of England was taken by his Protestant daughter Mary II and her husband William of Orange, but all of Ireland, except for obstinate pockets of resistance at Enniskillen and Derry, was held for the Catholic James by Tyrconnell, who, having purged the army of intransigent Protestants, commanded a force two-thirds of which was composed of Roman Catholics.

In March 1689, with the backing of the French King Louis XIV, James II came from France and landed at Kinsale, County Cork, with the French ambassador, a Lieutenant-General in the French army and a group of French, Irish, English and Scots officers. The King proceeded in triumph to Dublin, where a Roman Catholic-dominated parliament convened and resolved that the parliament of England could not legislate for Ireland. The administration's pursuance of a policy of catholicization alarmed the Protestant population who, above all, feared losing their property. A compromise was suggested by which Protestants would cede half their land to dispossessed Roman Catholics. In all but one county a Roman Catholic sheriff was appointed. The alarm of the Protestants grew. At the same time Roman Catholics clamoured for full redress; the Roman Catholic church was not, however, re-established, but all varieties of Christian worship were put on the same level. On the other hand the act of settlement was reversed and the confiscation of the majority of the land held by Protestants was sanctioned. The Jacobite army besieged Derry, which held out gallantly for over three months although the Protestant population and garrison were starving.

Despite his Continental involvement William III was obliged to intervene. A Williamite force led by General Schomberg landed in Ulster in August 1689 but, badly afflicted by disease, this army of 19,000 men made little progress. In March 1690 a further Williamite force of 6,000 infantry and 1,000 cavalry hired from the King of Denmark landed in Ireland. English, German and Dutch troops followed.

Sir Neil O'Neill, 2nd Baronet, Captain of Dragoons in the army of James II; he died in 1690 aged 32 of wounds sustained at the Battle of the Boyne. The portrait is attributed to Garret Morphey.

Finally, in June 1690, King William himself landed in Ireland with 15,000 troops in 300 ships.

A confrontation took place at a bend of the River Boyne, west of Drogheda, on 1 July 1690. The Williamites totalled about 36,000 men, the Jacobites about 25,000, including about 7,000 French; the Williamites were victorious. James, abandoning his supporters, fled to France. William took Dublin and marched west hoping to take Limerick, but its defenders resisted his siege. However, Marlborough landed in Cork with a Dutch and Danish force and, by taking Cork and Kinsale for King William, cut off the Jacobites' main route of supply and contact from France. The Dutch Williamite General, Ginkel, took Athlone, thus breaching the Shannon line held by the resisting Jacobites. In the ensuing confrontation of the two armies, each about 20,000 strong, at Aughrim in July 1691, the Jacobite commander was killed and the Williamites again won. In September the last Jacobite resistance crumbled with the surrender of Limerick to the besieging Williamites.

The total Williamite victory decided the balance of power and enabled the government firmly to cement the foundations of an enduring power structure in which the majority of the Irish population was excluded from any office of consequence and systematically degraded, while a Protestant minority enjoyed an administrative, social and cultural ascendancy.

The chaos and confusion of Tudor and Stuart Ireland resulted in the exodus of a number of Irish from their native country. Religious persecution and restriction of worship, political oppression, pestilence, war, economic depression, social dislocation, and the difficulty of pursuing higher education and spiritual training were all factors which induced emigration. In addition, a number of Irish were forcibly transported to the New World. At the end of the Stuart monarchy, following the Treaty of Limerick, the exodus reached its peak with the departure of thousands of Jacobite soldiers and their dependents.

Continuing in the missionary spirit of the early Irish Christian monks, there were Irish missionaries in the New World early in the sixteenth century. An Irish priest was teaching in the West Indies in 1525; later in the century a Limerick Jesuit served in Paraguay; and in 1597, Father Richard Arthur was pastor of St Augustine, Florida, the first Irish priest to serve in what is now the United States of America.

By the end of the sixteenth century the number of indigent Irish in France was sufficient to cause concern to the French authorities; the Irish colony was expelled from Rouen, and in 1606 the French government shipped two boatloads of Irish from Paris back to Ireland. After the defeat of the Irish at Kinsale many followed their leaders into exile on the Continent, mostly in France where the principal Irish colonies were in Paris, St Malo, Reims, Nantes and Bordeaux; but they also went to northern Spain, Portugal and Flanders, where there was a sizeable colony in Brussels. In that same decade 6,000 Irish swordsmen left to serve in the army of the King of Sweden. A report to the English court in 1614 gave the number of Irish soldiers serving the King of Spain in Spain and Flanders as 3,000, including 1,000 nobles.

The expulsions from the city of Galway provoked a further wave of emigration, mostly of merchants who set up in business on the Continent and in the West Indies. The exact number of Irish forcibly dispatched to the Caribbean islands by Cromwell is not known but it seems that it ran into thousands. Of the 12,000 Irish in the West Indies in 1669 some would have been transplanted and others emigrants recruited as contract workers to serve a period of from three to seven years, usually under very wretched conditions, until they redeemed their freedom. In the 1650s, during the Commonwealth regime, about 25,000 Irishmen went to serve in the armies of France and Spain. The government did not hinder their departure, counting it a blessing to be rid of so many potential enemies.

The most prominent Irish family on the Continent in the first half of the seventeenth century were the O'Neills, around whom Irish nationalist hopes centred. There were many colourful personalities, reckless, swashbuckling mercenaries, as well as a number of learned men, physicians and theologians. Luke Wadding, who founded the college for Irish Franciscans at Rome in 1625, was one of the most outstanding of Irish émigrés. This brilliant and energetic friar was born in 1588 at Waterford of a family of Old English stock. After preliminary studies in Ireland he was sent for further education to Portugal, where he decided to enter a Franciscan novitiate and was ordained priest in 1613. He served as president of the Irish College at Salamanca before going to Rome in 1618 as chaplain to the Spanish ambassador. Wadding spent the rest of his life in Rome, where his college, which he provided with an extraordinary library, became a centre of Irish patriotism. His diplomatic intervention enabled Irish soldiers serving in the Spanish forces to return to fight in Ireland in 1642, and he persuaded the Pope to send Cardinal Rinuccini to Ireland. In fact the Confederate Catholics, whose agent in Rome Wadding was, had hoped that Wadding himself would have been sent to Ireland as papal nuncio. He was also a prolific author, publishing 36 books including the *Annales Minorum* and a 12-volume edition of the works of Duns Scotus, which was continued by his brilliant nephew Father Bonaventure Baron, a native of Clonmel who spent most of his adult life in Rome, where he enjoyed the friendship and esteem of Popes Urban IV and

OPPOSITE *Burncourt, County Tipperary. The castle was built in 1641 by Sir Richard Everard, a Catholic Royalist, and burned out a few years later when it was attacked by Cromwell.*

FOLLOWING PAGES
LEFT *Askillana and the cliffs west of Louisburgh, County Mayo.*

RIGHT *The Victorian Gothic spire of the Roman Catholic church of St Joseph, Carrickmacross, County Monaghan, rises proudly above the town and its rural surroundings.*

Luke Wadding, Franciscan, priest, theologian and patriot, was one of the most brilliant minds of seventeenth-century Ireland; portrait painted in Rome by Carlo Maratta.

Alexander VII. A gifted writer and eloquent speaker, this Irish émigré Franciscan was recognized as an eminent humanist, historian, philosopher, theologian and poet. He was appointed historiographer to Cosimo de' Medici, Grand Duke of Tuscany, in 1676.

The final reversal of Irish hopes in 1691 provoked yet another and greater wave of emigration. About 10,000 Irish Jacobites left for the Continent; many were accompanied by their families, choosing a life of exile rather than degradation and penury at home.

OPPOSITE *Carbury Castle, County Kildare, the seat of the Colleys, ancestors of the 1st Duke of Wellington. The ruins of this fortified Jacobean strong-house are a gaunt reminder of the uneasy period of seventeenth-century settlement.*

5 Georgian Ireland

The gracious life-style of the new society rising to privileged prominence in the eighteenth century on the ashes of Gaelic Ireland, and after the eclipse of its old aristocracy, was lived in the cruel shadow of the penal laws passed in the reigns of William III and Anne to fetter the Roman Catholic majority of the population and impede its advancement. The bitter memory of this unjust discrimination has, unfortunately, prevented some Irish men and women from appreciating the culture of the new society or caring for its elegant architecture and arts, but the new society certainly enriched the multi-cultural national heritage, and left Ireland with precious monuments of a beauty which has outlived its own privileged term of existence. Just as Soviet Russia can cherish the opulent palaces of the Tsarist regime, built and luxuriously furnished at the expense of gross inequality and serfdom, so Ireland has come to realize that the monuments of an attractive but despised class, the Protestant ascendancy, are a precious legacy, a priceless and important part of the whole national heritage.

The penal laws

When William III undertook his campaign in Ireland he was anxious to maintain the support on the Continent of his then ally the Emperor. To secure the Emperor's approval William gave assurances that he would protect the Roman Catholic Irish from religious persecution and see that they were allowed the same degree of freedom as they had under Charles II. Thus he obtained the approval of the Emperor for his conquest of Ireland and, because of the alliance, the tacit approval of the Pope. In Ireland William promised the Roman Catholics a share in the administration, enjoyment of their estates, and half the church buildings in the country for their worship. But once free of his Roman Catholic allies on the Continent, William bowed to the Protestant lobby and reneged on all his promises. Over one million acres were confiscated, and the Roman Catholic population, far from being treated with tolerance, was subjected to the harsh restrictions of penal laws passed between 1702 and 1715.

The Roman Catholic hierarchy was sentenced to exile and all religious orders were banished from Ireland. Only the diocesan clergy were tolerated, and they had to register and provide bondsmen to vouch for their loyalty and obedience to the crown. In 1709 1,080 priests were registered. No Roman Catholic could be elected to the Irish parliament or hold public office; the Roman Catholics were disenfranchised, barred from university education in Ireland and even forbidden to teach. The penal laws also placed restrictions on land tenure which made it extremely difficult for any Roman Catholic to retain his family estate except with the connivance of Protestant friends.

The bigotry of the extreme Protestant faction in the reign of George I is illustrated by the extent of the Irish Privy Council's desire in 1719 to deter unregistered priests from entering Ireland surreptitiously: if apprehended, such priests were to be castrated. In the Lord Lieutenant's view, branding the culprits was not a sufficiently severe punishment. Therefore, along with the Lord Chancellor of Ireland, Alan Broderick, first Viscount Midleton, the Protestant Bishops of Meath and Clogher and others, he signed his name to these barbarous and alarming proposals and forwarded them to London:

> The common Irish will never become Protestant or well affected to the Crown while they are supplied with Priests, Friars etc., who are the fomenters and disturbers.... The Commons proposed the marking of every priest who shall be convicted of being an unregistered priest ... remaining in this Kingdom after 1st of May 1720 with a large 'P' to be made with a red hot iron on the cheek. The council generally disliked that punishment, and have altered it into that of castration which they are persuaded will be the most effectual remedy....

This awful bill was not, however, enacted, apparently because of advice from London, where diplomatic pressure in favour of Irish Roman Catholics was exercised by France, at that time an ally of England. The mere fact that such an atrocious measure was endorsed and urged by the Irish Privy Council is indicative of the climate of intolerance.

Despite the laws, pastoral activity continued. Unregistered priests resorted to such ruses as celebrating the Mass behind a curtain so that members of the congregation, if questioned, could explain why they could not identify the celebrant. The Mass was celebrated in hedgerows, in barns, in houses and among ruins. In the cities, where a Roman Catholic was able to fare better in trade than the landless countryman, the Roman Catholic meeting places were masked by private dwellings, shops, warehouses – or an inn, as in the case of the Dublin church still known as Adam and Eve's from the days when it was thus disguised. The Franciscans, the most zealous and persistent of the religious, continued an 'underground' ministry, and other orders also managed to maintain a presence despite the risks involved.

The expatriates

Rather than eke out a wretched existence in an Ireland disabled by penal laws, a continuous flow of ambitious young men left for the Continent, following the main exodus of the Wild Geese who went abroad *en masse* after the Surrender of Limerick. Those that were fortunate sent back to Ireland for their friends. While not a few rose to fame in their adopted countries, the majority spent their lives in hardship, knowing no other home than the camp. Many spilt their blood and lost their lives on foreign battlefields, in the Irish Brigades or as mercenaries in foreign service. At first King James II, at his court in exile at St Germain-en-Laye near Paris, where he died in 1701, then his son the Old Pretender, who was King James III to the Irish expatriates until his death at Rome in 1766, were the centre of Jacobite hope and loyalty. However, with the failure of the Rising of 1745 when Charles Edward (Bonnie Prince Charlie), the Young Pretender, attempted to regain the crowns of Ireland, Scotland and England for his father, the Jacobite cause began to wane. When Charles Edward became titular king on his father's death, the reigning Pope Benedict XIV, not wishing to incur the hostility of England, did not recognize his sovereignty, and by the time of his death at Rome in 1788 the Jacobite cause had become a pathetic memory.

Peter de Lacy, who had served in the defence of Limerick as a lad of 13, was undoubtedly the most successful of the Wild Geese who went into exile when the city was surrendered. Born in 1678 at Killeedy, County Limerick, he eventually entered the service of Peter the Great, rose to the rank of field-marshal, was created a Count, amassed a fortune and became Governor of Livonia and Estonia; he led the Russian army to victory against the Turks, and against the Swedes whom he expelled from Finland. Peter de Lacy's son, Maurice Francis, attained the rank of field-marshal in the Austrian army. A later Irish emigrant to Russia, Cornelius O'Rorke, born in 1736 in County Leitrim, married a grand-daughter of Peter de Lacy and became a major-general in the Russian army. Their son, Count Joseph O'Rorke, was one of the Russian generals who fought Napoleon; his portrait hangs in the gallery of heroes of that epoch in the Hermitage at Leningrad.

In the Austrian service Field-Marshal Con O'Donnell, son of Hugh O'Donnell of Larkfield, County Leitrim, became Governor of Transylvania; his brother John (1712–84) also rose to the rank of field-marshal in the Austrian army. Andrew O'Reilly, a native of Ballinlough, County Westmeath, another Irish field-marshal in the Austrian army, became Governor of Vienna in 1809.

Ambrose O'Higgins, whose family originated in County Sligo but who was born near Laracor in County Meath in 1720, went into the Spanish service as a military engineer in Chile and became Viceroy of Peru, where he died in 1801. His natural son Bernardo O'Higgins was the liberator of Chile and its first president. As commander-in-chief of the army, Bernardo O'Higgins appointed an Irishman, John MacKenna, born in 1771 at Clogher, County Tyrone, as his second-in-command. Several families in the Irish colony in Spain prospered. Alexander O'Reilly, born in 1730, became Governor of Louisiana in 1767 and subsequently commander of the Spanish forces in the eastern Pyrenees. Members of the O'Reilly family and of other prominent Irish émigré families – O'Donnells, O'Briens, O'Neills and Kindelans – are still in Spain today. The senior descendant of the O'Neill chiefs of Clandeboye, the senior branch of the ancient royal house of Ulster, is a Portuguese nobleman, Jorge O'Neill, living in Lisbon.

In France, where the greatest number of Wild Geese settled, many attained titles, fame and fortune. Among the most notable was Henry Clarke (1765–1818), Duke of Feltre, Marshal of France and Minister of War under Napoleon I, whose father had gone to France from County Kilkenny and there married the daughter of an officer in the Irish Brigade. Oliver Harty, Baron de Pierrebourg, born at Knockany, County Limerick in 1746, a cousin of Henry Clarke, took an active part in the French Revolution and was a distinguished general in the army of Napoleon I. Edmè Patrice Mac Mahon, Duke of Magenta, Marshal of France and its president from 1873 to 1879, was the grandson of John Baptist Mac Mahon, an Irish physician from Limerick who settled in Burgundy after completing his studies at Reims. Thomas O'Gorman, born in 1732 at Castletown, County Clare, became an intimate of Louis XV; he married a wealthy French heiress, but after a luxurious life in Paris lost his estates in the Revolution and returned to Ireland, where he died. A native Irish speaker, the Chevalier O'Gorman was also an enthusiastic Irish antiquarian. Richard Hennessy of Ballymoy, Killavullen, County Cork, who went to France in 1740 at the age of 20, after serving in the army settled at Cognac, where he established the famous Hennessy distillery. The Bordeaux branch of the Lynch family from Galway, from which came John Baptist Lynch, mayor of Bordeaux and a Peer of France, is now extinct, but their name is perpetuated in the famous claret Château Lynch-Bages and the lesser-known Château Lynch-Moussas.

The colonial society

The new society in Ireland, which successfully supplanted the older ones although it was English-oriented, soon diverged from the pattern of the mother country. The tastes and fashions were essentially those favoured in England, with a time lag of a few years, but subtle variations developed; the buildings had a distinctively Irish look, some furniture could not be anything but Irish, and silver objects were produced peculiar to the Irish workshops. The life-style of the nobility, the gentry and the lesser fry of the new society, too, developed an idiosyncratic quality, so that although

ABOVE *Count Joseph O'Rorke, son of an emigrant from County Leitrim, was one of the Russian generals who defeated Napoleon.*

OPPOSITE LEFT *Count Maurice Francis de Lacy, who attained the rank of field-marshal in the Austrian army.*

OPPOSITE RIGHT *Ambrose O'Higgins, born in humble circumstances in County Meath, entered the Spanish service and became Viceroy of Peru.*

LEFT *Henry Clarke, Duke of Feltre, Marshal of France and Minister of War under Napoleon I, was the son of Irish émigré parents.*

BELOW *Field-Marshal Count John O'Donnell, a native of County Leitrim, who with his brother the Governor of Transylvania rose to high rank in the Austrian Imperial service.*

they may have seemed very English to their tenants and neighbours of old Irish stock, they stood out as Irish in the eyes of the English visitors.

It would be easy to exaggerate the real or imaginary differences between the gentry in England and the people we now refer to as the Anglo-Irish (in the eighteenth century that term had not been coined). Romantic novelists, raconteurs, supercilious visitors from England, and the Anglo-Irish themselves, have contributed to a store of legends about a reckless, feckless, profligate, high-living, free-spending, wild, charming, inter-bred, eccentric Anglo-Irish gentry. Real differences, however, did exist. In certain ways the Anglo-Irish gentleman landowner was more similar in his life-style and outlook to a Virginia or Carolina planter across the Atlantic than to an English squire across the Irish Sea; the relationship between the Irish landowner and the wretched Roman Catholic peasantry, living barely at subsistence level, was more like that of the planter with his slaves than that of the English squire with his labourers. The analogy can be taken so far as to include the attitude of contempt mingled with tolerant amusement with which both the planter and the Anglo-Irish landowner regarded the drolleries of their respective serfs, Sambo and Remus in America, Paddy and Mick in Ireland.

Like the Southern planters, too, the Anglo-Irish gentry fathered many illegitimate offspring with girls and women of the underprivileged class. The natural children born of these unions, unlike the bastards of an English aristocrat or squire, usually bore their father's name. This and the acceptance of irregular unions and their issue may be seen as a relic of the older Gaelic social system, with its plural matrimony, unorthodox matrimonial situations and concubinage, the children of which invariably bore the paternal family name. Marriage within a kinship network was usual in rural Ireland where Protestants were thin on the ground. Marriages between first cousins were quite frequent. In rural Munster, by the end of the eighteenth century most husbands and wives of the Protestant gentry shared some common ancestry.

One habit of the Anglo-Irish gentry which was distinct enough and widespread enough to provoke frequent comment by English visitors was their consumption of wine. 'Nine gentlemen in ten in Ireland', remarked Lord Chesterfield, 'are impoverished by the great quantity of claret which, from mistaken notions of hospitality and dignity, they think it is necessary should be drunk in their houses.' A traveller in Ireland about 1750 noted that at every little inn one found Bordeaux claret and Nantes brandy. The philosopher Bishop Berkeley, himself a member of the Protestant ascendancy in Ireland, noted that while many an English gentleman with an income of £1,000 a year did not have wine in his house, this could hardly be said of a gentleman in Ireland who had only £100 a year. The diary of a country clergyman, the Revd John Nixon, Rector of Innismacsaint, County Fermanagh, covering 1769–71, bears out these comments. Sixteen people at a Saturday afternoon dinner party at Mr Nixon's rectory (dinner was taken at about 4 pm) drank 14 bottles of claret and four bottles of port; 13 guests stayed on for supper and drank four more bottles of claret, two more of port and a bottle of whiskey. Eight at dinner on another occasion drank nine bottles of claret, two of port and one of madeira. One Sunday after church Mr Nixon, his curate, and one other guest, drank nine bottles of claret and two of port among the three of them; after tea and prayers they drank a further bottle each of both claret and port. Yet there is nowhere any comment in the diary that this was unusual or excessive.

Many landlords entertained their tenantry once a year or on some special family occasion. When Lord Ely entertained 120 in the hall of Castle Hume Manor in 1770 they drank 19 gallons of rum in a punch, six gallons of whiskey and two barrels of ale, while claret and port flowed liberally in the parlour.

Sirloins of beef, legs of mutton, ham, poultry, game, cod with oyster sauce, pickled oysters, lobster, cheese, pies, cakes, jellies and sweetmeats graced a gentleman's table. The staple food of the peasantry was potatoes and their fare usually included a thin gruel called stirabout, oatcakes, and, for those lucky enough to have a pig to slaughter, an occasional piece of bacon. Tea was a luxury beyond the means of the poor. Tenant farmers lived better than the peasantry and could afford to keep a hog, a sheep or a few chickens for their own kitchens.

That sharp, silver-tongued observer of eighteenth-century society in Ireland, Sir Jonah Barrington, divided the gentry of the country into three categories: half-mounted gentlemen, gentlemen every inch of them, and gentlemen to the backbone. The 'half-mounted' he compared with what would have been the yeomanry in England, descendants of the small grantees of the Tudor, Cromwellian and Williamite settlements, but who in Ireland were occasionally admitted into the society of the great landowners while also on intimate terms with their own servants. According to Sir Jonah, a man of this class usually had good, clever horses, wore buckskin breeches and well-greased boots, and brandished large thong whips loaded with lead at the butt end, with which they were always ready to horsewhip some wretch or even knock his brains out.

Certainly, the lines of demarcation between the middle and upper classes were less distinct in Ireland than in England. The possession, though only as a leaseholder, of a couple of hundred acres, put a farmer on the fringe of the gentry in Ireland, where class barriers were vague and easily breachable.

Movement down the social ladder could be as brisk as movement upwards. The younger sons of a landed gentleman, unless they did well in the church, the army, the law, or in trade, or else hooked a wealthy heiress, soon found themselves at farming level. Then their younger sons, landless and penniless, were faced with the prospect of emigration to the new colonies or of a miserable existence in Ireland, although, as Protestants, they could always hope to fare better than the population at large and could seek the patronage of their better placed connections.

Holy orders in the Established Church could provide the way to social improvement, but, for a minister without other means and with a large family, it could herald social decline for his children and grandchildren. Two random examples illustrate this. The Revd Gethin Crone, born in 1728, Rector of Doneraile, County Cork, was connected with several prominent county families, in particular to the local magnate, through his mother who was a niece of Arthur St Leger, first Viscount Doneraile. During Gethin Crone's incumbency of Doneraile parish the great mansion, Doneraile Court, was occupied by his close kinsman Hayes St Leger, fourth Viscount Doneraile, Privy Councillor and member of parliament for Doneraile. Yet the Revd Gethin Crone's grandsons became small farmers, and the youngest, Robert Crone, was a servant employed by a local family of gentry to whom he was closely related, the Smiths of Carker. On the other hand, for the family of Oscar Wilde's mother, the Elgees of Dundalk, the Church provided an upward stepping-stone. Two brothers, stonemasons from Staindrop, County Durham, in the north of England, settled in Dundalk in the 1730s, where they found employment as a result of the building boom. One of them was able to send a son to Trinity, and this son, John, who became Rector of Wexford and Archdeacon of Leighlin, married into a prominent Wexford family; among his grandchildren were Sir Robert John le Mesurier McClure, the explorer of the North West Passage, the poetess 'Speranza', who married Sir William Wilde and was mother of Oscar Wilde, and three major-generals in the British Army.

The law as a profession could be lucrative for a clever practitioner because disputes over wills, settlements and land tenure proliferated. Henry Deane Grady, born in 1765, the descendant of an ancient Irish family in County Limerick which had kept its lands by becoming Protestant and identifying with the establishment, was such a successful lawyer and KC that he was able to find titled husbands for four of his five daughters.

Between men in occupational trade in Ireland and those who qualified as gentry, the division was nebulous. Again and again in a succession of deeds a given person will be described, say, as 'builder' and later as 'gentleman'; as 'linendraper', and later as 'gentleman'; or as 'cutler', and later as 'gentleman'. Or even more surprisingly, as in the case of Thomas McCann (or Macan) of Armagh, born in 1717, as 'soap-boiler' and then as 'gentleman'; in due course he served as Sovereign of Armagh and fathered two high sheriffs of County Louth and a major-general, Commander of Fort William, Bengal.

The most successful and spectacular *parvenu* was William Conolly, a man of native Irish ancestry and the son of a modest innkeeper at Ballyshannon, County Donegal, who joined the establishment bandwagon and, as a lawyer, amassed a colossal fortune by dealing with the forfeited estates after the Williamite confiscations. Elected member of parliament for Donegal, he went on to become Commissioner of the Revenue in 1709 and Speaker of the Irish House of Commons in 1715. By the end of his life Speaker Conolly was the richest man in Ireland and had built the grandest mansion in the country.

The colonial taste and fashion

Among the buildings designed in the Classical, Baroque, Rococo and Neo-Classical styles imported from Britain and the Continent are some which have a definitely Irish character. Architectural historians found this to be so marked in the adaptation of the Palladian villa plan in Ireland that they named the style Irish Palladian.

The dearth of architects and artists in Ireland left room for ambitious incomers to acquire lucrative practices. While some, like Edward Lovett Pearce, came from England, a number of the most talented came from the Continent, so we may attribute some of the peculiar qualities of Irish architecture and decorative arts to a Continental influence which did not filter through England. Three outstanding architects in eighteenth-century Ireland were the Italian Alessandro Galilei, Richard Castle (or Cassel), who came from Saxony, and Davis Ducart (d'Aviso de Arcort), a citizen of Sardinia, apparently originating from Piedmont or Savoy. The Francini brothers from Italy, virtuoso stuccodores, embellished houses built by these Continental architects and set the pace for Irish stucco workers. Another eminent stuccodore in Ireland was Bartholomew Cramillon, a French or Walloon Huguenot refugee who had been in Italy; his masterpiece is the decoration of the chapel of the Rotunda Hospital, Dublin.

As soon as he could afford to, and sometimes sooner, a gentleman would commission an architect or builder to erect a mansion as an expression of the distinction of his rank and refinement. The houses of the first two decades after the Surrender of Limerick demonstrate a considerable time lag from their prototypes abroad. An example is Stackallan House in County Meath, built about 1716 by one of the victorious Williamite generals, Gustavus Hamilton, first Viscount Boyne. It resembles an English country house of the reign of Charles II. The town mansion built by the Uniacke family at Youghal, County Cork, between 1706 and 1715, now known as the Dean's House, is in the style of Dutch domestic architecture of at least 30 years before. Shannongrove, a delightful house in County Limerick built in 1709, also shows Dutch influence and has an old-fashioned, high-pitched roof. The old Custom House, Dublin, of 1707, designed by an Irish-born architect, Thomas Burgh, had a double-sloped hipped roof with dormers.

The arrangement devised by Palladio for his Venetian clients, who required an elegant country villa which was also the centre of a functional farm, naturally found favour in Ireland. The answer was a central residential block linked by curtain walls to pavilions which could accommodate stables and staff quarters while presenting

The Allegory of Faith, the work of the Walloon Huguenot stuccodore Bartholomew Cramillon, in the Rotunda Hospital Chapel, Dublin.

to the onlooker an elegant and pretentiously expansive facade. This is the arrangement used with consummate skill by Galilei in 1722 for William Conolly at Castletown, County Kildare, where the architect achieved a *parvenu*'s dream without vulgarity or ostentation. This grandiose house is now cared for by the Irish Georgian Society; it is open to the public, who can admire the superb Rococo stucco decoration by the Francini brothers in the staircase hall, the cantilevered stone staircase of 1760, made by the sculptor Simon Vierpyl who had worked in Rome, the long gallery with wall paintings in the Pompeian manner by Thomas Riley, 1776, and the two-storey entrance hall and the curving wings with Ionic colonnades designed by Edward Lovett Pearce, who took over the work after Galilei. A restaurant is now installed in the great vaulted kitchen in the west pavilion.

Richard Castle, who followed the tradition of Galilei and Pearce, was the architect of such splendid Palladian mansions in Ireland as Russborough, County Wicklow, begun in 1741 for Joseph Leeson, later first Earl of Milltown (now, with its magnificent collection of pictures, open to the public, thanks to the philanthropy of its

Published according to Act of Parliament

L. Tudor delin.

Parr Sculp.

A Prospect of the Custom House, and Essex Bridge, DUBLIN.

Veüe de la Douäne, et Dupont d'Essex, a DUBLIN.

twentieth-century owner, Sir Alfred Beit, Bart), and Powerscourt in the same county, built in the 1730s for Richard Wingfield, later first Viscount Powerscourt, which was unfortunately gutted by fire in 1974. Richard Castle designed many other Irish houses in his prolific career; Frenchpark, County Roscommon, a Palladian winged mansion of 1729, has been demolished, but many examples of his work survive. The first Duke of Leinster's great town mansion, Leinster House, is now the seat of the Irish parliament, Dail Eireann; Ballyhaise, County Cavan, with an oval saloon, is now an agricultural college; Hazlewood, County Sligo, has become the Irish offices of an Italian firm; Bellinter, County Meath, is a convent and used as a retreat and conference centre; Ardbraccan in the same county, built about 1734 for the Bishop of Meath, is still in private residential occupation. A much smaller but perfectly designed house in County Longford, Ledwithstown, now sadly derelict, may also have been Castle's work. Two storeys over a basement with a three-bay facade and without wings, it is more typical of what the average country gentleman could afford.

The architect of Crosshaven House, County Cork, built in 1769 for the Hayes family, is not known; architectural historians have pointed out that he must have based his design on Isaac Ware's *Complete Body of Architecture* which contains a similar design for a house at Bristol in England. A three-storey, five-bay house flanked by free-standing pavilions, Crosshaven House, coming at the very end of the Irish Palladian phase, embodies the desire for importance and elegance on a restricted scale. In the 1770s at Kilcarty, County Meath, the architect Thomas Ivory built a two-storey, five-bay, glorified farmhouse with single-storey, two-bay wings, still in the Palladian tradition. Frequently Irish builders worked from English architectural pattern books.

Davis Ducart, who also built winged mansions in Ireland, introduced in his work elements of the Baroque style which flourished in his own country. Ducart must have seen in Piedmont the extraordinary work of the royal architect Filippo Juvarra, who moved from designs in which he favoured static, sharply defined spaces, to more fluid concepts influenced by stage design. In Ireland Ducart's known works include Castletown Cox in County Kilkenny, built in 1767 for the Archbishop of Cashel. Here the central block, whose design is derived from that of Buckingham House in London, built in 1703, is linked by wings, which are arcaded on the garden front, to pavilions crowned with cupolas. Another of Ducart's houses, Kilshannig, County Cork, built in 1765–6, contains superb plasterwork by the Italian Francini brothers; but the stuccodore employed at Castletown Cox was an Irish artisan, Patrick Osborne, who also worked in Waterford. The ability of a Waterford architect, John Roberts, to create a Baroque effect, which he did magnificently in the forecourt of Curraghmore, County Waterford, may indicate that he had trained or travelled abroad, or possibly that he had worked with Ducart.

A number of expert Irish stuccodores were working in Ireland after the Francini brothers. The most famous, Robert West, decorated the staircase hall of 20 Dominick Street, Dublin, in the early 1760s, Richard Chapell Whaley's house at 86 Stephen's Green, and others. West specialized in birds in high relief. His friend Michael Stapleton was another eminent stuccodore, whose delicate work can be seen at Mount Kennedy, County Wicklow. Provincial Irish stuccodores imitated the work of the virtuosi; an example is the plasterwork at Mount Juliet, County Kilkenny, executed in the 1780s in the manner of Michael Stapleton.

The dining-room of Mount Juliet, County Kilkenny.

Drishane, Castletownshend, County Cork, an unpretentious but delightfully serene two-storey, six-bay, weather-slated house on a rectangular plan, was built near the end of the eighteenth century by a successful Cork merchant whose previous residence on his inherited lands had been an uncomfortable converted tower-house. This reflects the real situation of many, even well-placed, scions of colonial society whose addresses may sound grandiose on documents but who were not infrequently still living in medieval towers in the latter half of the eighteenth century.

The 'half-mounted' gentlemen, with less capital than the rest (if they had any at all beside what they could raise on a mortgage or acquire by a judicious marriage), also wanted a fine house instead of the bleak discomfort of a tower or the simplicity of a plain, long, low, thatched farmhouse, one room deep. The solution they found by the end of the eighteenth century was a neat, economical villa, usually graced with a high-faluting name. Advertisements for the building of a villa in the last decade of the century offered a three-bedroomed, box-shaped house with accommodation for maidservants in the garrets and a kitchen in the basement, for as little as £762. We may compare this with the £696 paid to the stuccodore Patrick Osborne for the plasterwork alone at a grand house like Castletown Cox. A smarter three-bay, four-bedroomed house with a fancier facade could be had for £1,057, including outbuildings such as a coach-house, kennels, dairy, turfhouse and harness room. A seven-bay, eight-bedroomed villa with an Ionic portico cost £2,900. An impressive gateway at the entrance to the avenue was priced between £150 and £350. A large number of these simpler houses built for the gentry and clergy in the late eighteenth century survive in Ireland. Behind a simple facade they often have well-proportioned, high rooms, symmetrically disposed, and good Classical features.

By the end of the century the rich were commissioning buildings in the Neo-Classical style. Irish-born architects had appeared, notably Francis Bindon, Thomas Ivory and John Morrison, but the leading architects of Neo-Classicism were again talented incomers, this time Englishmen, Thomas Cooley and James Gandon. They were followed by two Irish-born rivals, Francis Johnston and Sir Richard Morrison, who designed in both the Classical and Gothic styles. The famous English architect, Robert Adam, was commissioned to design rooms at Headfort, County Meath, and to remodel Castle Upton, County Antrim. The equally celebrated Wyatt sent over designs for rooms at Curraghmore, County Waterford, Abbeyleix, County Leix, and Westport House, County Mayo, where his interior work may be seen as the house is open to the public; he also made early designs for Slane Castle, County Meath. All these, of course, were residences of the very rich who could afford the services of the great.

The Mussenden Temple, a domed rotunda in the grounds of Downhill, County Derry, was erected as a memorial by the Earl-Bishop of Derry, a confirmed Italophile. The architect, a Cork builder, Michael Shanahan, based his design on the Roman Temple of Vesta. Lord Charlemont, like the Earl-Bishop, visited Rome and was enthralled by the architecture of antiquity; on his return to Ireland he commissioned the leading English architect of the day, Sir William Chambers, to build him a town house in Dublin and a small pleasure house at Marino outside the city; the sculptor Vierpyl was brought from Rome to work on it. This expensive and obsessively architectural casino is now a National Monument.

Besides these extravagances Ireland has other fine Neo-Classical houses on a grand scale. Caledon, County Tyrone, was designed by Thomas Cooley in 1779 for James Alexander, subsequently first Earl of Caledon, who had amassed a fortune in India. It was later enlarged by another eminent English architect, John Nash, who added single-storey flanking pavilions with domes and redecorated the splendid oval drawing-room. The prodigious Wyatt was mainly responsible for Castlecoole, County Fermanagh, built in the 1790s for the first Earl of Belmore, and now maintained by the Northern Ireland National Trust; it is open to the public, who can admire its unusually perfect Grecian interior as well as the impressive facade with its giant pedimented portico, the deeply recessed colonnades with fluted Doric columns and the Doric pavilions. James Gandon, brought to Ireland at the behest of the first Earl of Portarlington, designed a country house for him, Emo Park, a private residence in County Leix. It was considered an architectural rival to Castlecoole. A giant pedimented Ionic portico adorns the seven-bay facade, and another was added on the garden front in the 1830s; the great coffered dome above the magnificent rotunda was not completed until about 1860. Ballyfin, a later, lavishly decorated Classical mansion, also in County Leix, which owes its present appearance to rebuilding in the 1820s, is now a Patrician College. It seems to have been

View of the Four Courts, looking down the River Liffey
DUBLIN

ABOVE *The Four Courts, Dublin, designed by James Gandon and begun in 1786.*

OPPOSITE ABOVE *The Custom House, Limerick, designed by Davis Ducart and built during 1765–9, was his first known commission in Ireland; it presages his ability to create a grandiose façade on a small scale.*

inspired in several respects by Emo Park and also has a rotunda with a coffered dome. Ballyfin's immense Ionic portico graces a vast 13-bay front.

Cooley and Gandon, Ireland's leading Neo-Classical practitioners, designed a number of superb public buildings. Dublin owes to Gandon's genius several of its proudest and most conspicuous buildings. His magnificent Custom House was begun in 1781; the sculptor Edward Smyth decorated the elegant south front on the Liffey with a series of keystone heads which represented the rivers of Ireland and the union of Britannia and Hibernia. In 1785 Gandon added the handsome Corinthian portico to the Parliament House, now the Bank of Ireland. The Four Courts overlooking the Liffey, incorporating an early building by Cooley, were designed by Gandon and begun in 1786. His 1795 design for the impressive King's Inns was not executed until 1802; 50 years later the building was restored. The present O'Connell Bridge is a nineteenth-century reconstruction of Gandon's Carlisle Bridge of 1792. Dublin's City Hall of 1769 was designed by Thomas Cooley.

The Irish-born Francis Johnston, who with Sir Richard Morrison dominated the architectural scene in the early nineteenth century, was equally at home with Classical or Gothic design; he built excellent country houses in both styles, the most spectacular of his Gothic houses being Charleville Forest, County Offaly, built in the first decade of the nineteenth century; his most impressive Classical house is Townley Hall, County Louth, designed in 1794 for Blayney Balfour, with a singularly beautiful stair in a rotunda lit by a glazed dome. Dublin's General Post Office, with its Ionic portico, completed in 1818, is the work of Francis Johnston, who also designed the Gothic-style Chapel Royal in Dublin Castle, completed in 1814.

While country-house owners often vacillated between Classical and Gothic, the former was favoured for public building throughout the country. Morrison's Court-

*Emo Park, County Leix, was begun
c. 1790 to the designs of James
Gandon; his only essay in the
country-house style, it was
something of a rival to Wyatt's
more famous Castlecoole.*

*Carlow Courthouse, designed by
Richard Morrison.*

Oxmantown Mall, Birr, County Offaly, an elegant late Georgian terrace.

house at Carlow is one good example of this, the austere Doric courthouse at Dundalk, County Louth another. The Classical tradition died hard in Ireland. The glory of eighteenth-century Georgian Dublin was emulated with diminishing success until the middle of the nineteenth century, holding its own against other styles. Oxmantown Mall at Birr, whose terraced houses date from the 1820s, is a fine example of provincial Georgian; this style may be seen at Armagh, where it was still very fashionable in the 1840s, at Tralee, at Limerick, at Waterford, and in countless smaller towns throughout the country, where a row of such houses built for the doctor, the solicitor, or a genteel dowager often grace the townscape.

The medieval towns, like Kilkenny, which grew in a cluster, differ greatly in their plan from the large number of small towns and villages of the seventeenth and eighteenth centuries. Unlike the English village, usually clustered about the green and the parish church, the Irish village is often strung along a single broad street. Where the villages and small towns were part of a landlord's estate and he planned their layout, a gracious town plan was the result; examples are Westport, County Mayo, Castlecomer, County Kilkenny and Strokestown, County Roscommon, where the landlord planned a main street wider than the Ringstrasse in Vienna, then reputed to be the widest in Europe.

By the middle of the eighteenth century the Established Church recognized that it was in possession of three or four times as many ruined church buildings as functional ones. To remedy this situation and to promote the influence of the Protestant Church by aiming to have one erected in every parish or union of parishes, the Irish parliament voted annual grants from 1777 to a body called the Board of First Fruits to subsidize a church-building programme. From an annual parliamentary grant of a few thousand pounds a year, out of which the Board usually made grants of £500 for a new church, the parliamentary grant rose to £60,000 a year between 1810 and 1816. Over a million pounds passed through the Board's hands between 1800 and 1823, of which almost half was spent on church-building. Not surprisingly, then, many of the little Protestant parish churches of rural Ireland, built in a simple Gothic revival style and now often in disuse, date from that period.

As long as the Irish parliament still met there, Dublin had all the glamour of a

Fishamble Street 'Musick Hall', Dublin.

capital. Its entertainment – fashionable assemblies, concerts, pleasure gardens, theatres and musical halls – attracted grandees and minor gentry alike. The top attractions were the viceregal balls and receptions at Dublin Castle. As well as these and other such orthodox entertainments as the first performance of Handel's *Messiah* in Dublin in 1741, the Smock Lane Theatre and the Music Hall in Fishamble Street, masques and private parties, there were illicit attractions like Peg Plunket's notorious high-class brothel, the Citherean Temple on Pitt Street.

Only the very rich could afford a Dublin mansion like Belvedere House with its lavishly decorated Diana Room, Apollo Room and Venus Room, or Lord Aldborough's house with its private theatre. The reasonably rich lived in elegant squares of tall terrace houses. But most of the minor gentry took temporary lodgings in the capital.

Painting In that century of peace after the Surrender of Limerick, when so many houses were built, there was a demand for fashionable furnishings and decorative items. Portraits headed the list and were the most popular items of interior decoration. The leading portraitists in the reign of George I were Hugh Howard and Charles Jervas, both of whom had studied in Rome. James Latham, whose background was Anglo-Irish, studied in Antwerp and was a talented portrait painter, but unfortunately he died at the age of 50 so his legacy of work is limited. His contemporary Stephen Slaughter, an Englishman who painted in Ireland, had also studied in Flanders, and in Paris. In the next generation the painter Nathaniel Hone, of Anglo-Irish background, went from his native country to work in England.

The drawing schools founded by the Dublin Society in the mid-eighteenth century did much to improve and encourage painting by providing tuition in drawing, arranging exhibitions, and awarding prizes. Hugh Douglas Hamilton, whose small, oval pastel portraits hang in many of the more important country houses in Ireland, was a pupil of the Dublin Society's drawing schools. Many country gentlemen, however, commissioned portraits from mediocre itinerant artists; the patrons were more interested in an approximate likeness than in a work of art.

Despite the magnificence of Ireland's scenery, landscape painting developed slowly. A number of competent landscape artists emerged, however, from the Dublin Society's schools in the second half of the eighteenth century, the most eminent being George Barret, and landscapes flourished with the growth of Romanticism. In the next generation the most remarkable landscape painters were the Roberts brothers and William Ashford, an Englishman who lived and worked in Ireland for about 60 years. James Barry, the son of a Cork builder who painted scenes from mythology, history and the Bible as well as portraits, was by far the most illustrious painter that Georgian Ireland produced, but he made his highly successful career in England after a sojourn in Italy.

To have one's miniature painted was very popular with the gentry and, because it was not expensive, it made an excellent gift and memento. So many young officers had their likenesses painted in miniature for their family or a lady-love that the miniaturists took to preparing the uniformed busts in advance, to which they could quickly add the actual sitter's face. Adam Buck of Cork (1759–1833) was one of the most renowned miniaturists of his day and also executed small full-length portraits in pencil, crayon and watercolour. Even more prolific in Ireland was his brother, Frederick Buck, a capable miniaturist.

A period of affluence after the Napoleonic Wars which brought hard cash into Ireland (in return for foodstuffs supplied to the troops and in the form of soldiers', sailors' and officers' pay) coincides with a peak in portrait commissions of all kinds. When George IV visited Ireland in 1821, the first monarch to do so since William III, many country ladies acquired new jewels and finery to wear when they came to Dublin for the celebrations, which were only slightly marred by the King's discomfort with diarrhoea. A portrait of the lady dressed in her best to hang in the dining-room commemorated the visit for the family, the neighbours and posterity.

LEFT *Jane Newman of Dromore, Mallow, County Cork; an example of the work of the miniaturist Frederick Buck.*

RIGHT *Portrait of Bridget, née Finucane, wife of Lt-Col. John Cullen, JP, of Skreeny, County Leitrim, painted at the time of George IV's visit to Dublin.*

Furniture

Lion mask, a detail from an eighteenth-century Irish table.

An Irishness can be discerned in some of the furniture and silver made in Georgian Ireland; like the house designs, although basically inspired by English models they have definite idiosyncratic features. This national style in furniture, if it can be called that, began to emerge in the late 1720s and 1730s. A set of chairs which, according to the inscription on one, 'Maher, Kilkenny 1740 Fecit', were made in Kilkenny, are in the Queen Anne style, fashionable in England 20 or 30 years earlier, but they also reveal Dutch influence – Maher may have been trained by or worked with one of the Dutch craftsman settlers, or perhaps he had seen chairs brought from Holland to Kilkenny Castle.

In the 1750s and 1760s Irish craftsmen were making sidetables, card tables, seats and other items for domestic use, many of them in imported dark West Indian mahogany, which they carved with low-relief decoration; this included grotesque masks which reach back far into Celtic tradition. Dublin was the centre of fashionable furniture-making. Because of the predilection for high-living, eating and drinking, dining-room furniture was particularly in demand. By the end of the century the Irish tradition had waned, and locally made furniture resembled imported furniture and illustrations in English pattern books.

Glass and silver

LEFT *A Dublin-made George II helmet-shaped creamer, c. 1740.*

CENTRE *A Dublin-made cream jug in the form of a goat, c. 1790.*

RIGHT *Decanter made at Waterford between 1783 and 1799 by the firm of Penrose; it is cut with slices and flutes and engraved with their mark, a quill pen and a rose.*

In the first three decades after the Surrender of Limerick Irish silver generally followed the plain traditions of Anglo-Huguenot workmanship and design. The established churches required only the simplest vessels, and the gentry, struggling to consolidate their hegemony and at best to build a comfortable dwelling, did not patronize the silversmiths beyond the strict limit of their requirements. A demand for domestic silver for the new houses towards the middle of the century was met by Irish silversmiths who manufactured objects with vernacular characteristics – flat-chased Rococo scrollwork, for instance, and individual shapes such as the helmet-shaped creamer, and the dish-rings sometimes called potato rings. In the last quarter of the eighteenth century there was a marked increase in production, and with it designs peculiar to Dublin, Cork and Limerick; a technique called bright-cut was employed for much of the silverware of this period.

In 1751 the Round Glass-House in Dublin claimed to be the only glass factory in the country. Glass manufacture began in Belfast and Cork in the 1770s and in Waterford, whose name is now internationally known for glass, in 1783. Beautifully blown and cut clear glass was produced in considerable quantity in Waterford and

Sculpture

Cork, especially between about 1800 and 1820, wine glasses, decanters, claret jugs, candlesticks and butter-coolers being the most in demand.

Sculpture, for which Irish craftsmen had long been famous, was confined in the early eighteenth century, as it had been in the seventeenth, mostly to funerary monuments and a little architectural decoration. Within the limits of tomb sculpture there are examples of exuberant, elegant workmanship. The tomb in the Protestant parish church at Kilnasoolagh, County Clare, of Sir Donat O'Brien, who died in 1717, is reminiscent of the Baroque monuments of Rome in the preceding century. Its sculptor, William Kidwell, who had trained in London under a master of English Baroque, executed other fine monuments in Ireland. Many simple Protestant churches have delicately sculpted Classical memorials on their walls, elegant Grecian urns, cartouches and entablatures, frequently embellished with the heraldic device of the deceased and an eloquent obituary. Rural sculptors did their best with simpler standing tombstones for patrons of modest means; their work, often no more than an inscription carved in relief with rather primitive symbols of the Passion or the Resurrection, nevertheless has its own charm.

The leading figure sculptor in Ireland in the eighteenth century, John Van Nost, came to Ireland from England, as did the virtuoso Simon Vierpyl who had also lived in Rome. Ireland's best native figure sculptor, Christopher Hewetson, came from a settler family in County Kilkenny. Although he lived and worked in Rome he remained in touch with the Irish grandees who made the grand tour, and with the émigré Irish colony there which included a few artists. Hewetson's monument to Provost Baldwin in Trinity College, Dublin, was sculpted in Rome. The name of Edward Smyth, born in 1749 in County Meath, has already been mentioned in connection with the Dublin Custom House. Smyth, trained by Vierpyl, was a fine sculptor, excelling in Neo-Classical decoration; he was followed in this tradition by his son John. The Classical style persisted even more obstinately in Irish sculpture than it did in architecture. The most ardently Classical of all the

BELOW *The sculptor Hogan was commissioned to make this memorial in St Isidore's, Rome, to the painter Amelia Curran who died in 1847. She was the daughter of the celebrated jurist and orator, John Philpot Curran.*

RIGHT *A putto extinguishing a torch on the tomb of Cardinal Rezzonico in the Church of San Nicola in Carcere, Rome, sculpted by Christopher Hewetson.*

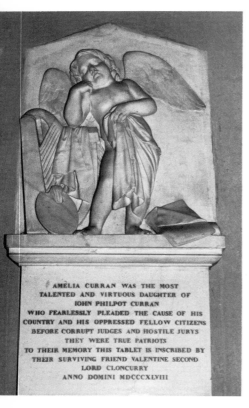

AMELIA CURRAN WAS THE MOST
TALENTED AND VIRTUOUS DAUGHTER OF
IOHN PHILPOT CURRAN
WHO FEARLESSLY PLEADED THE CAUSE OF HIS
COUNTRY AND HIS OPPRESSED FELLOW CITIZENS
BEFORE CORRUPT JUDGES AND HOSTILE JURYS
THEY WERE TRUE PATRIOTS
TO THEIR MEMORY THIS TABLET IS INSCRIBED BY
THEIR SURVIVING FRIEND VALENTINE SECOND
LORD CLONCURRY
ANNO DOMINI MDCCCXLVIII

Irish sculptors was John Hogan, a native of Cork, who spent 25 of his working years in Rome. A Roman Catholic, working after Catholic Emancipation, Hogan tended to express this in his art through the medium of nineteenth-century Catholic piety and triumphalism. His contemporary, Patrick MacDowell, a native of Belfast who went to live and work in London, was also a fine sculptor but very influenced by the sentimentality of his time.

Creative writing
Despite the restrictions on the Gaelic world, the ancient traditions of story-telling and poetry persisted, and courteous acknowledgments were made by the Anglo-Irish literati to the truly native literary culture. Swift, who viewed both English and Irish society as a critical outsider, although he was born in Dublin and educated at Kilkenny and Trinity College, Dublin, translated *O'Rourke's Feast* from the Irish. Oliver Goldsmith, whose background was also that of the Protestant ascendancy, wrote an essay on the Irish poet Carolan. While both Swift and Goldsmith were in the Augustan tradition, the importance of the Irish element in their work cannot be ignored. The literary legacy of Swift can be discerned over a century after his death in the work of W. B. Yeats, who in fact acknowledged it, of James Joyce, and in this present century, of Patrick Kavanagh. Swift, who frequently felt condemned to a life in Ireland without preferment and against his will, produced, among his lesser-known work, delightful vignettes of Anglo-Irish life in his time. He wrote part of *Gulliver's Travels* at Quilca, County Cavan, where he stayed as a guest of his friend the Revd Thomas Sheridan, grandfather of the Dublin-born playwright Richard Brinsley Sheridan. Swift recalled the discomfort of the house at Quilca in his poem, 'The Blunders, Deficiencies, Distresses and Misfortunes of Quilca', which describes its cold, its draughts and the negligent service.

Brian Merriman, a teacher of mathematics in County Clare, has left us his wonderfully rich, earthy *Midnight Court*, written in Irish, which reminds us that poets of the ancient native tongue were not silenced by the gravity of political events and social change. As late as the end of the eighteenth century we have the powerful *Lament for Art O'Leary*, composed by the dead man's wife Dark Eileen O'Connell in the rich tradition of women poets in the Irish language. Eilis Dillon's translation fully conveys its urgent, passionate depth of feeling in the last stanza.

> I struck my hands together
> and I made the bay horse gallop
> as fast as I was able,
> Till I found you dead before me
> Beside a little furze-bush.
> Without Pope or bishop,
> Without priest or cleric
> To read the death-psalms for you,
> But a spent old woman only
> Who spread her cloak to shroud you –
> Your heart's blood was still flowing;
> I did not stay to wipe it
> But filled my hands and drank it.

The first writer from an eighteenth-century Irish Catholic background to achieve international fame was Thomas Moore, whose work was praised by Goethe. His highly successful *Irish Melodies*, dedicated to 'The Nobility and Gentry of Ireland' are rich with plaintive lines like:

> As vanquish'd Erin wept beside the Boyne's ill-fated river
> She saw where Discord in the tide, had dropp'd his loaded quiver
> 'Lie Hid', she cried, 'ye venom'd darts, Where mortal eye may shun you,
> Lie hid – for oh! the stain of hearts that bled for me is on you.'

or,

> Oh Arranmore, lov'd Arranmore,
> How oft I dream of thee,
> and of those days when, by thy shore,
> I wondered young and free.
> Full many a path I've tried, since then,
> through pleasure's flowery maze,
> But ne'er could find the bliss again
> I felt in those sweet days.

Moore's poetry echoes the theme of mourning for the vanished glories of ancient Ireland, which courses through the slow rebirth of Irish nationalism.

The collapse of Jacobite aspirations after the failure of Bonnie Prince Charlie's rising in 1745 signalled a relaxation of anti-Catholic apprehension and, in the second half of the century, Protestant fears of Roman Catholic power diminished in Ireland. Slowly the Roman Catholic Irish began discreetly to reassert themselves without exciting antagonism. At Cork, Dublin, Limerick, Waterford and Armagh, for example, circumspect places of worship were fitted up. A most interesting eighteenth-century Roman Catholic church survives at Waterford; dedicated to St Patrick, it is in a side alley, outwardly indistinguishable from the secular buildings around it. Originally the entrance was even more discreet because its approach, between shops since demolished, was narrower than the present lane. Inside, the galleried church resembles a little theatre, arranged to accommodate a large congregation in a limited space. In a rural area under the watchful eyes of the Protestant administration it would have been difficult to build such a church in the 1760s, but the earlier harsh application of the penal laws was becoming increasingly rare. By the end of the century most of the anti-Catholic laws had been repealed or were not invoked. Roman Catholic freeholders with holdings valued at above 40 shillings a year obtained the right to vote in 1793.

The growth of tolerance

Scions of the seventeenth-century Protestant settler families, born in the more relaxed atmosphere of the mid-century, after more than 50 years of peace and relative prosperity, were the third or fourth generation to be born in Ireland. Like their contemporaries in Colonial America in the 1770s, whose revolution and breakaway from England was to influence them, a number of young men of Anglo-Irish Protestant background identified themselves more with Ireland and Irish problems than with the causes and attitudes of the mother country of their forefathers. Further factors which affected this generation in Ireland were the liberal ideas of the European Age of Enlightenment and the revolutionary philosophy and ideals emanating from France. It was these enlightened Protestants who were the moving spirits in urging reform and awakening the dormant nationalism of the Irish masses.

At parliamentary level Henry Grattan progressed from urging the lifting of restrictions on Irish trade to pressing successfully for Irish legislative independence; he introduced the repeal of the act by which all but money bills passed by the Irish parliament were subject to revision by the English Privy Council, and the repeal of the English Declaratory Act of George I's reign which asserted the right of the English parliament to legislate for Ireland. Grattan also attempted to relieve the distress of the Irish masses which had provoked the Whiteboy disturbances. He boldly opposed the corrupt machinery of Dublin Castle and demanded an enquiry into the sale of peerages. In supporting the Roman Catholic Relief Bill of 1792 he declared that, 'The removal of all disabilities is necessary to make the Catholic a freeman and the Protestant a people,' but his resolution of 1796 to allow Roman Catholics to sit in the Irish parliament was defeated by 143 to 19. A further defeat in 1797 provoked Grattan's resignation – he explained that he approved neither of the revolutionary United Irishmen nor of the repressive conduct of the government. Grattan saw that the government's policy would draw Ireland inevitably into union with Great Britain and violate her fragile liberty. After the Union, which he had strenuously opposed, Grattan continued to urge Roman Catholic emancipation in the London House of Commons.

But there were more radical spirits abroad than Grattan – men eager for change and impatient of legislation. Theobald Wolfe Tone, born in 1763, was the son of a Dublin coachmaker, himself the son of a County Kildare farmer. Tone's first bold exploit was to elope with Matilda Witherington, the 16-year-old grand-daughter of a rich clergyman. While still in his twenties he became interested in political issues and formulated ideals which are best expressed in his own words: 'To subvert the tyranny of our execrable government, to break the connection with England, the never-failing sources of all our political evils ... to assert the independence of my country ... to unite the whole people of Ireland, to abolish the memory of all past dissensions.'

United Irishmen   At the time, the Scots Presbyterians in Ulster expressed warm approval of the French Revolution, and in Belfast the storming of the Bastille on 14 July 1789 was celebrated enthusiastically. Tone, realizing that the Protestants of the Established Church of Ireland would not willingly surrender their privileged status, grasped the importance of uniting the dissenters, Ulster Presbyterians, and the Roman Catholics. To promote this he went to Belfast in 1791 and organized the nucleus of a society to unite Irishmen of every religious persuasion, in order to obtain, as he put it, 'a complete reform of the legislature, founded on the principles of civil, political, and religious liberty'. The Society of United Irishmen grew rapidly. Among the early adherents in Dublin were the colourful and popular James Napper Tandy, son of a Dublin tradesman, and Archibald Hamilton Rowan, a wealthy landed proprietor from County Down; together they raised two battalions of supporters in the capital, each 1,000 strong, with green uniforms and harp buttons. Thomas Addis Emmet, a doctor of medicine turned barrister, who eventually became a director of the United Irishmen, defiantly took the oath of the society in open court. Thomas Russell, a former army officer and one of Tone's earliest associates, was responsible for the northern party with Samuel Neilson, the son of a Presbyterian minister from County Down, and Henry Joy McCracken, a Belfast textile manufacturer. John Keogh was the leader of the Roman Catholic party.

The United Irishmen favoured and hoped for armed intervention in Ireland by France, England's enemy, but the northerners expected more from a national rebellion. Tone went to France under an assumed name in 1796 to plead for French assistance, and a French expeditionary force of 43 ships carrying 15,000 soldiers sailed for Ireland in winter 1796. Rough weather scattered this fleet and prevented those that reached Bantry Bay from landing. Tone joined a second expedition in 1797 in which the Dutch also took part, but this had to be abandoned because of bad weather.

Lord Edward Fitzgerald, one of the 17 children of the twentieth Earl of Kildare (later first Duke of Leinster), after serving in the Irish parliament and supporting Grattan's reform minority, veered towards a revolutionary ideology. He was cashiered from the British Army for his audacious toast at a banquet in Paris in 1792 when the company, at his command, drank to the abolition of all hereditary titles. In Ireland Lord Edward joined the United Irishmen who, by 1797, claimed to have a quarter of a million armed followers at their command and openly avowed their aim of an independent Irish republic. Thomas Addis Emmet, more cautious than Lord Edward, advised holding back until the French landed before coming out in rebellion, but frustration at the thwarted French expeditions, combined with growing resentment at repression, coercion and outrages at home, exasperated the patience of the United Irishmen.

The 1798 rising

On 19 May Lord Edward, who was to have commanded the insurrection planned for 23 May, was apprehended. He died in gaol in Dublin from wounds sustained when he was arrested. Before the end of May armed rebel parties rose in Dublin and Meath, and also in Kildare where they attempted unsuccessfully to take the town of Naas, the garrison at Clane, and the town of Monasterevan. Without a commander, undisciplined, angry mobs of rebels resorted to savage acts of retribution, murder and robbery. Panic-stricken Protestants fled from their homes. Dublin was placed under martial law. At Carlow, where rebels attempted to take the town, the military set fire to houses in which the rebels were hiding; about 80 houses were burnt and several hundred rebels were burned alive. On 24 May around 30 men suspected of sympathy with the rebels were summarily shot by the military without trial at Dunlavin, County Wicklow; coals were heaped on the fires of resentment as the flame of rebellion reached Wicklow and Wexford where, with thousands armed, it reached even more frightening dimensions. Enniscorthy, one of the most important towns, fell to the rebels led by Father John Murphy, a Roman Catholic priest; by 30 May they had marched into Wexford, where they released Bagenal Harvey, a Protestant landowner, from gaol and appointed him their commander-in-chief. In the reigning climate of fear stories of bloodthirsty massacres ran rife. Accounts were exaggerated on both sides, but there is no doubt that some rebels perpetrated horrible crimes in their excitement to exact retribution for the floggings, burnings and cruel measures of repression that had been inflicted by loyalists on followers of the United Irishmen. Roman Catholics were led to believe that the Orange Order, founded in 1795 to combat popery and defenderism, was in fact dedicated to the extermination of all Roman Catholics, so they butchered Protestants whom they suspected of Orangist sympathies. Interested parties fanned the flames of sectarian bigotry.

Early in June rebellion broke out in the north, in County Antrim, but the republicanism of Presbyterian United Irishmen was being eroded by the growth of the Orange movement and the news of atrocities committed by Roman Catholics in the south. At Ballinahinch, County Down, the military defeated a strong rebel force led by Henry Monroe, a linendraper from Lisburn who had to contend with dissension between Presbyterians and Roman Catholics under his command as well as widespread desertion. Paradoxically the Monaghan Militia, which fought on the government side, was an almost exclusively Roman Catholic regiment, while the majority of the rebels were Protestants. Those who were captured were hanged immediately.

Within a month, amid disgraceful cruelties on both sides, the rebellion had been suppressed in Wexford. Before the end nearly 100 Protestant prisoners were massacred on Wexford Bridge by rebel pikemen. The victorious government troops retaliated by slaughter and indiscriminate burning of houses in their hunt for the rebels, 65 of whom were also hanged from Wexford Bridge.

A French force of 1,000 men under General Humbert landed at Killala, County Mayo, later that summer after the popular rising had been put down. They arrived too late and in the wrong place. Napper Tandy, who landed on Rutland Island off the Donegal coast in September, raised an Irish flag there and then learned of the defeat of Humbert's expedition. Tone, who sailed with another French force of 3,000, was captured when it encountered a powerful English naval squadron off the Donegal coast. He was sentenced to execution for high treason, but died in gaol of a self-inflicted wound before the sentence was carried out. Russell, McCracken and other United Irishmen leaders were executed; Napper Tandy escaped abroad, as did Samuel Neilson who died in the United States.

The Act of Union

The terror generated by the rebellion crushed tolerant attitudes and created a climate in which it was possible to ram the Act of Union through the Irish parliament in 1800. A number of prominent pro-Unionists were rewarded for their vote with a peerage. The Dublin parliament was abolished and its powers vested in the London parliament of the United Kingdom of Great Britain and Ireland which came into being on 1 January 1801.

Pitt, the English Prime Minister whose cabinet had engineered the Union, wished also to grant full Roman Catholic emancipation. This policy won him considerable Catholic support, including that of many of the hierarchy. However, George III and the bulk of English public opinion opposed emancipation and Pitt resigned three months after the Union came into being.

Robert Emmet, the younger brother of Thomas Addis Emmet, and a fellow student at Trinity College of the poet Thomas Moore, had an interview with Napoleon in Paris in 1802. He was again promised help to secure Irish independence but it was not forthcoming. Emmet published a proclamation of a national government in Dublin and mounted a private plot with this aim, but it was foiled and he was arrested and hanged.

Catholic emancipation

It was an Irish Roman Catholic aristocrat of old Gaelic stock who eventually won emancipation for the Roman Catholics some years after the Union, when the worst fears, animosity and tension had abated. Daniel O'Connell came from a County Kerry family, many of whose scions had followed the trail of the Wild Geese. The most successful was an uncle, Lieutenant-General Count Daniel O'Connell, who served both in the French army and the Irish Brigade and died in France a rich man; he bequeathed much of his property to his nephew Daniel, the champion of emancipation in Ireland. This younger Daniel, after studying in France and London, was called to the Irish bar on the day of Lord Edward Fitzgerald's arrest, 19 May 1798; he was one of the first Roman Catholic barristers to be allowed by the Relief Act of 1793. O'Connell became the dominant personality in Irish political life. To procure Roman Catholic emancipation he organized the masses. His Catholic Association founded in 1823 had a branch in almost every parish in Ireland. By organizing a 'Catholic rent', whereby members of the association paid a monthly due of one penny, he stimulated the interest, involvement and political maturity of the people. Although it was uncertain whether, as a Roman Catholic, he would be able to take his seat in the House of Commons, O'Connell stood for County Clare in 1827 and was elected. Due to his tireless, single-minded effort and the massive popular agitation which he organized, the dream of emancipation at last became a reality in 1829, and with it O'Connell became a national hero. He had always been an opponent of the Union, which he described as 'odious' and 'abominable', and from 1830 he was able to turn his attention to urging its repeal; he was arrested for this on charges of conspiracy, but the case was dropped. In fact O'Connell was adamant in working for repeal through parliamentary reform, but he realized the value of non-violent agitation. In 1840 he founded the Repeal Association on the lines of the old Catholic Association. In 1843 he was arrested on charges of sedition and found guilty. He was sentenced to a year's imprisonment but did not have to serve it as the House of Lords reversed the judgment. O'Connell lived through the end of the Georgian era and acclaimed the accession to the throne of the young Queen Victoria, but he did not achieve repeal of the Union.

6 Disaster and Recovery

In a country where poverty and malnutrition were endemic, the partial failure in 1845 of the potato crop, the staple diet of the poor, was ominous. Daniel O'Connell, now past 70, informed the House of Commons of the prevalence of poverty, famine and disease in Ireland in a speech in February 1846, and moved for a committee to be set up to cope with relief of the suffering. A year later, on 8 February 1847, when the famine was already reaping its grim toll, O'Connell spoke in the Commons for the last time, appealing to parliament to save Ireland from disaster. 'She is in your hands – in your power,' he pleaded with the assembled MPs. 'If you do not save her she cannot save herself.'

O'Connell himself was ailing. His doctors recommended a change of climate and he left for Italy, where he died that spring. Meanwhile in Ireland, where his body was returned for a hero's burial, the conditions of the people had never been worse, nor had they ever seemed so hopeless.

Social conditions

It would be false to think of that underprivileged Irish proletariat as an isolated or unique phenomenon in the Europe of the 1840s. In rural Italy and rural Spain, for example, and in the industrial towns of England and south Wales, people struggled under appalling social and economic conditions. Certain elements of the Irish situation differentiated it from other countries and made it more dramatic, but the greatest difference was in the change of social structure which was to follow.

The population of Ireland grew alarmingly from under 5 million around 1800 to over 8 million by 1840. Of this 8 million, 700,000 – almost one in ten – appear in the 1841 census returns as landless labourers; there were a further 300,000 cottiers with holdings of under five acres. It was among these classes that the rate of population growth was the highest, and their state of distress was critical before the catastrophic famine of the 1840s. They lived in primitive, one-room mud cabins, often without window or chimney. Such dwellings made up about 40 per cent of the total in 1841. The overcrowding was shocking; the average of 11 persons to a one-room cabin, according to the returns of the 1861 census, indicates that some of these wretched hovels must have housed 20 people or more, along with any domestic animals they were lucky enough to possess. Under conditions like this it is not surprising that diseases such as typhus and cholera spread rapidly.

Poverty and distress were most severe in the rural west, which had the highest percentage of landless and near-landless peasants and the poorest land. A description of conditions in a parish in western Donegal in 1837 is gruesome; the schoolmaster reported that the 4,000 inhabitants of the parish, all Roman Catholics, owned only 10 beds and less than 100 chairs between them; whole families huddled together naked or covered in rags, sleeping on the ground which was strewn with straw or

OPPOSITE Irish Emigrants Waiting for the Train, *painted by Erskine Nicol.*

rushes. There was only one cart and one plough in the parish and miserably few farming implements.

It is startling to discover that despite prevailing distress there was a high rate of literacy in Ireland, even allowing for some exaggeration in census returns: 47 per cent of the population over five years of age in 1841 and 53 per cent in 1851 claimed to be able to read; by 1911 88 per cent of the population was literate.

Despite the grinding poverty of the masses, social gatherings were enlivened by a contrasting gaiety. The fiddler, the piper and the story-teller still provided entertainment at weddings and wakes, at fairs, at markets, and at popular places of pilgrimage where the enjoyment sometimes reached such giddy excess that a scandalized church hierarchy stepped in and suppressed the gathering, as they did in the case of the annual pilgrimage to Glendalough. Father Mathew's temperance crusade did much to reduce the heavy drinking which had become a major social problem, but one that was barely recognized until his organized efforts to combat it. Both beer and whiskey were cheap, and there was no shortage of *poitín* available from illicit stills throughout the country which evaded the excisemen. Despite the temperance movement, drunkenness remained rife, alcohol providing an escape from grim reality.

The famine

When the potato crop was struck by blight in 1845 the potato was the staple food of one-third of the population of Ireland, and a major element in the diet of many more. In that year some of the crop was saved, but the blight attacked in 1846, again, but less severely, in 1847, and again in 1848. As a result, between 1845 and 1850 about 800,000 men, women, and children (one-tenth of the population) perished from hunger and disease. The death-roll comprised almost exclusively the poorest section of the population – the landless labourers and the cottiers. The workhouses, already inadequate, were overfilled. By the summer of 1847, although emergency soup kitchens had been set up to dole out a daily ration to about 3 million peasants, people were still dying on the roads and in the ditches, where they dropped, sick and exhausted, as they tried to reach help or a port from which to emigrate.

Emigration

The drop in population in those famine years was dramatic. Between the census of 1841 and that of 1851 the number of inhabitants declined by 20 per cent; in addition to the famine's death toll of around 800,000, about 1,500,000 people left Ireland. Emigration continued throughout the century; each succeeding 10-yearly census recorded a further decline in the population, beginning with a drop of 11.5 per cent between 1851 and 1861. Between the famine and 1914 5,500,000 people left Ireland; in those 60 years the population was reduced to just over half what it had been when the famine struck. As well as the continuing emigration, a pattern of later marriage and celibacy developed in the second half of the century, with a consequent drop of 20 per cent in the birthrate; from 35 per 1,000 before the famine it dropped to 28 per 1,000 in 1870. The population decline in the west was consistently higher than the national average – 28.8 per cent in Connacht and 22.5 per cent in Munster between 1841 and 1851, compared with the national average of 19.9 per cent. The national decline between 1841 and 1911 was 46.4 per cent; in Connacht it was 57 per cent and in Munster 56.8 per cent. In Ulster where industrial development, especially in the Lagan valley, provided needed jobs, the fall was only 33.8 per cent over the same period. The population of Belfast actually increased from 100,000 to 400,000 between 1850 and 1914.

The census figures for the second half of the century provide a clear picture. They show the depopulation of the poorer lands in the west, and everywhere a radical change in the social structure, with a sharp decrease in the labouring population, an even sharper decrease in the cottier population – verging towards the elimination of the one- to five-acre holdings – and the number of small farmers with five to fifteen acres cut by half; the number of inhabitants with over fifteen acres actually increased by 20 per cent, despite the overall decline in the population.

The demise of the Irish language

It has been claimed that the deaths and emigration of the famine years were the cause of a radical reduction in the use of the Irish language. In fact the decline in the percentage of Irish speakers began long before the famine, but was accelerated

This cartoon from the Weekly Freeman *is a comment on the depopulation of rural Ireland. Old Molly tells the Recruiting Sergeant: '... Don't ye know well that ye have driven away, to Americay, all the fine strong men that used to be in these parts, and left only me to take yer shillin'.'*

by the higher proportion of deaths and emigrations in the rural west where the highest percentage of Irish speakers lived. Before the famine about half the population spoke Irish, many speaking at least some English and a number being bi-lingual. By 1851 only a quarter of the population spoke Irish at all and only five per cent spoke it exclusively. In the second half of the century the use of Irish dropped drastically in the face of the need to speak, read and write English, the language of the government, the law, the armed forces and business, and a necessary one to the prospective emigrant. A study of the 1901 census returns shows overwhelmingly that the post-famine generations throughout most of the country were solely English-speaking. Most of those who spoke Irish as well as English were over 60. Irish-speaking areas persisted on the Atlantic seaboard, with a few small inland pockets, notably in the counties of Waterford, Meath, Louth and Cork.

Young Ireland

OPPOSITE *Lucan, County Dublin. In the nineteenth century, social conscience finally dictated the building of adequate housing for workers. This terrace, beside a textile mill overlooking the Liffey, is a good example.*

FOLLOWING PAGES *Clare Island and the north coast of Clew Bay from Polgloss.*

In October 1842 three enthusiastic adherents of O'Connell's Repeal Association launched a newspaper to publicize their views and the crusade for Repeal. One – Thomas Davis, a barrister – was a Protestant; the other two were Roman Catholics – Charles Gavan Duffy, a self-educated journalist from Ulster, and John Blake Dillon, the son of a prosperous Mayo farmer with business connections. Dillon had studied for the priesthood at Maynooth, but left to enter Trinity College; there he met Davis and, like him, became a barrister. All three were under 30. They shared not only the same political views on Repeal but were also linked by their romantic nationalist ideology. With other ardent young men who shared their opinion that the nation in itself was a spiritual entity, they came to be known as the Young Ireland group. Davis was also a poet and expressed the lofty idealism of the Young Irelanders in verse. Jane Francesca Elgee, later Lady Wilde and the mother of Oscar Wilde, was a partisan of Young Ireland. Under the pen-name 'Speranza' she published her prose and verse in *The Nation*, which soon had a circulation of 10,000 and a reader-

ship of 200,000 or more. The last issue of *The Nation* before it was suppressed in 1848 contained an article by Speranza urging the young men of Ireland to take up arms, and this was used by the government in its unsuccessful prosecution of Charles Gavan Duffy on a charge of sedition. Davis's views on the necessity of forging an Irish national identity, regardless of creed, ancestry, or background, are expressed in one of his verses:

> What matter that at different shrines
> We pray unto one God?
> What matter that at different times
> Our Fathers won this sod?
> In fortune and in name we're bound
> By stronger links than steel;
> And neither can be safe nor sound
> But in the other's weal.

The Young Irelanders cherished a hope of regenerating the spirit of Ireland. Romantic as that aim may seem, it is a fact that their high-minded, uncompromising nationalism did much to generate a revival which, as it developed through the nineteenth century, embraced not only politics but also literature and the arts.

Post-famine influences

Three influences marked the search for an Irish identity in the second half of the century. Their results can be seen in the political, cultural and social patterns of the new Ireland which was to emerge. The Roman Catholic church was opposed to Fenianism, but republican nationalism came to associate Roman Catholicism with its own identity, a Roman Catholic background being considered more essentially and distinctly Irish than a Protestant one. The attitudes of the cultural and social-political nationalists and of the Roman Catholic hierarchy sometimes coincided, but they were essentially divergent influences and often conflicted.

One influence was cultural nationalism, a legacy of the founders of the Young Ireland movement. It was manifested by a Celtic renaissance, a revival of literary and artistic interest in ancient Ireland and in Gaelic mythology and folklore. The nationalist attitude of its practitioners ranged from the cautious to the passionate. As a cultural movement it was the most vigorous that Ireland had known for a thousand years, and it left the country enriched with the works of a galaxy of internationally acclaimed writers, poets, dramatists and artists.

A second influence was that of social nationalism, the legacy of James Fintan Lalor and those who supported his views that only a new social contract and radical reform of land tenure could remedy the evils of poverty, distress and oppression. The immediate heirs of these social reformers were the founders of the more radical Irish Republican Brotherhood, the Fenians, who demanded a republic totally separated from England. Their political ethos is still present today in Ireland.

A third influence was that of the Roman Catholic church and its hierarchy, which became a powerful force under the implacable leadership of one of the ablest churchmen of the last century. After 18 years as rector of the Irish college in Rome, Paul Cullen returned to Ireland in 1848 to take up his duties as Archbishop of Armagh and Roman Catholic Primate; in 1866 he became Ireland's first Cardinal. With unswerving determination he enforced a policy which brought Irish Roman Catholicism strictly into line with Roman discipline, and transformed a convivial, loosely organized church with little effective sway over the lives and morals of its members into an austere, institutionalized ultramontane church with a strong episcopate, able to exercise an inflexible and puritanical authority. This influence has waned, but a statement by a Roman Catholic bishop still receives more publicity in the national press and causes more discussion in secular circles in Ireland than in any other country.

OPPOSITE *Honan Chapel, Cork. The furnishings, decoration and vestments of this chapel at Cork University are superior examples of Celtic Revival art. Eight of the beautiful stained glass windows are by artists of An Tur Gloine and eleven by Harry Clarke, of which this one, dedicated to St Declan, depicts in the lower panel his legendary meeting in Italy with St Patrick.*

The national cultural revival

Even before the rise of the Young Ireland movement promoted a 'national' art, writers and painters in Ireland had been attracted by Irish subjects and the local scene. Nathaniel Grogan, who died in 1807, painted scenes which accurately portrayed peasant life, with such titles as *The Itinerant Preacher*, *The Wake* and *The Country Schoolmaster*. Another Irish genre painter, John George Mulvany (1766–1839), painted delightful interiors of farm kitchens and inns which are informative in their attention to detail. This interest in rural life and customs was the very substance of the writing of William Carleton, the son of a peasant family near Clogher, County Tyrone, whose *Traits and Stories of the Irish Peasantry* was published in the 1830s. The sketchbooks of Samson Twogood Roche, an accomplished and fashionable miniaturist who lived near Youghal, are filled with sketches of local peasant life, in contrast to the smart silk- and velvet-swathed gentry of his professional commissions. When the novelist Maria Edgeworth had to stay for some time in Connemara because of the illness of a travelling companion, she recognized a unique opportunity for social observation in a part of Ireland where a vanishing life-style persisted among landowners and peasantry alike.

Subject paintings too reflect budding romantic nationalism, but they go beyond it to explore the awakening of the social conscience. Fairs and pilgrimages began to attract the attention of painters. Joseph Peacock's *Festival of St Kevin at The Seven Churches, Glendalough* was exhibited in 1817. Joseph Patrick Haverty's *O'Connell at the Clare Election of 1828* is a straightforward subject painting recording an event of enormous national and popular importance; his *Limerick Piper* (often called 'The Blind Piper') reflects nostalgia for this aspect of Gaelic life and for the Gaelic past, while his *Father Mathew Receiving a Penitent Pledge-Breaker* is a subject with a social message. Interest in the country's antiquities resulted in the foundation in 1841 of the Archaeological Society of Ireland. An unusually early instance of antiquarian interest in things Celtic and, moreover, on a popular level, is to be seen in the churchyard at Ahenny, County Tipperary, where the tomb of Mary Dempsey, who died in 1802, is inscribed with her name and residence in Irish, in Ogham script, as well as in English.

OPPOSITE *'Going to Cork by way of Fermoy' from the sketchbook of Sampson Twogood Roche, c. 1831, shows a local farmer driving his pig to Fermoy market; the inscription implies that he will go on to Cork to spend the proceeds of the sale.*

LEFT *Tombstone with Ogham inscription to the memory of Mary Dempsey who died in 1802 at Ahenny, County Tipperary.*

BELOW The Wake, *painted by Nathaniel Grogan, shows the traditional gathering on a death.*

Painting

Against this fertile background Thomas Davis proclaimed the necessity of 'high art', an art which would contribute to the rebirth of a high-minded, ennobling national spirit. In *The Nation* he wrote, 'We entreat our artists as they love their country, as they owe it a service, as they pity its woes and errors, as they are wroth at its sufferings, and as they hope to share and aid in its advance, to use this opportunity of raising the taste and cultivating the nationality of Ireland....' Davis even suggested subjects for painters, ranging from *Niall and his Nine Hostages, St Patrick Brought Before the Druids at Tara* and *Shane O'Neill at Elizabeth's Court* to ones that were frankly and provocatively nationalist in the context of contemporary events.

Frederick William Burton (1816–1900), son of Anglo-Irish gentry from County Clare, was a friend of Davis and other Young Irelanders who, although he did not share their political views, took a deep interest in Irish history, legends and folklore. He was also a friend of the painter and antiquarian George Petrie, whose *Ecclesiastical Architecture of Ireland* was published in 1845, and with whom he travelled about the country. Burton pointed out to Davis that a national art could not be forced. He himself contributed to its development with such paintings as his *Blind Girl at the Holy Well* and *The Aran Fisherman's Drowned Child*.

Daniel Maclise (1808–70), a Cork shoemaker's son, was encouraged in his career as an artist by the antiquarian author Thomas Crofton Croker, whose book *Fairy Legends* he illustrated. He was commissioned to illustrate Mr and Mrs S.C.Hall's *Ireland: Its Scenery, Character, etc.*, published in London in three volumes in 1841–3, and also an edition of Thomas Moore's immensely popular *Irish Melodies*, published in 1845. In *The Origin of the Harp* he illustrates Moore's poem of that title; its vision of the origin of Ireland's native music is at once romantic, nostalgic and sensual, and it must be considered a landmark in the artistic revival, although it is now a lesser-known work than Maclise's great *Marriage of Strongbow and Eva*.

Architecture

The antiquarian researches of Petrie stimulated architects working in Ireland to search for examples in the country's architectural heritage from which they could borrow elements to introduce an Irish dimension in their designs. William Bardwell, the architect of Glenstal Castle, County Limerick, may have been advised and influenced by the Earl of Dunraven, an antiquarian friend of the owners, in his use of Hiberno-Romanesque detail; one doorway, executed in 1841, is a copy of the doorway in Killaloe Cathedral. Generally, it was the earlier and more individual round towers that attracted the attention of the architects.

J.J.McCarthy, an architect sympathetic to the Young Ireland movement, was praised by its leaders for his prolific output of Gothic Revival Roman Catholic churches, in many of which he used elements from Irish medieval churches and abbeys. His Roman Catholic parish church at Kilmallock, County Limerick, dedicated to St Peter and St Paul, incorporates a number of elements from the nearby ruined medieval Dominican friary. It was McCarthy who amended and completed the design for the Roman Catholic cathedral at Armagh, begun by Thomas Duff of Newry. McCarthy's successful Gothic work in the tradition of A.W.Pugin (whose cathedral at Killarney he completed after Pugin's death in 1852) can be admired at several cathedrals and many churches.

Under the influence of the Pugin school, which associated the Roman Catholic liturgy and tradition with Continental Gothic, the Catholics in Ireland abandoned the Neo-Classical style which they had strongly favoured in their first burst of emancipation church-building. Pugin was the architect of several Gothic Revival Roman Catholic churches built in Ireland in the late 1830s and the 1840s, and also of the Mercy Convent at Birr, County Offaly, with its attached three-storey round tower at one corner, complete with conical roof. In 1848, a small Protestant church was built with an attached round tower, the Church of Ireland chapel in the

OPPOSITE
The Origin of the Harp, *painted by Daniel Maclise.*

grounds of Old Court, County Down. W.H.Lynn's Church of Ireland parish church of St Patrick at Jordanstown, County Antrim, built 20 years later, represented an attempt at a revival of a Hiberno-Romanesque church in its entirety, inspired by Teampuill Finghin at Clonmacnoise and complete with round tower. Some serious historical research went into the designs for the stained glass windows at Jordanstown; an ancient Irish crozier in the British Museum was used as a model for St Patrick's crozier, and the border ornamentation is based on Celtic Christian decoration in the *Book of Durrow*.

Writing

The nineteenth-century literary revival in Ireland might easily have foundered on the rocks of chauvinistic parochialism. But there were writers who were able to transcend propagandism and sentimentalism. Stimulated by scholarly research into Ireland's past, an imaginative interest in its ancient traditions, and an awareness of the contemporary literary trends of realism and naturalism, they published works which won international acclaim and rightly have a place of importance in the literature of the English language.

The poet and antiquarian Sir Samuel Ferguson and the translator and historian Standish James O'Grady, both Protestant Unionists but lovers of Celtic Ireland, furnished inspiration and a body of information for later writers. William Butler Yeats (1865–1939) recognized his debt to these two, as did George Russell, who acknowledged that O'Grady's *History of Ireland* had kindled to life all that was Irish in him. It was, however, W.B.Yeats himself who made the greatest contribution to the literary revival by guiding it, giving it direction, strength and force, and by steering it firmly away from narrow-minded nationalism and conventionalism. Yeats insisted that an Irish national literature could exist which would be no less Irish in spirit for being written in English, or for recognizing the value of foreign literary influences. He embodied his ideals in his own verse and fiction, which has an

ABOVE LEFT *W.B.Yeats.*
ABOVE RIGHT *Oscar Wilde.*

essentially Celtic quality. Today we remember Yeats principally as a great poet, but his role in the development of Irish literature as a critic and counsellor should not be forgotten.

Two years younger than Yeats was George Russell (1867–1935), a man of wide interests and remarkable talents who shared many of Yeats's opinions. Russell, known as AE, had a flair for discerning talent in young writers. Among those he recognized and encouraged were James Joyce, Sean O'Faolain and Austin Clark.

Yeats, aware of the advantages of the stage as a vehicle for publicizing his ideology and as a means of reaching a large audience, worked tirelessly to create what he intended to be a national theatre. He had the support of, among others, the novelist George Moore, the aesthete Edward Martyn, and Lady Gregory. They all shared a Connacht background but were not always in agreement about the choice of plays. Of the coterie it was Lady Gregory who became Yeats's closest friend, ally and collaborator, and the success of the theatrical project, which found a home at the Abbey Theatre in 1904, is largely due to her unswerving loyalty and support. Lady Gregory's County Galway home, from which she made the expeditions into the countryside which she called 'folkloring', became more than a literary salon; it was a gathering place, a haven for her many brilliant friends and protégés. One was John Millington Synge; another, Edward Martyn, who lived a few miles away; Yeats bought a neighbouring tower, as did Oliver St John Gogarty. Philistinism and disregard have combined to wreak the decay of Lady Gregory's house, Coole Park, but one can still wander in the grounds and see where some of Ireland's most brilliant men carved their initials on a tree.

Yeats's *Countess Cathleen*, the Abbey Theatre's first production in 1899, was not the only play to provoke anger from the audience or controversy among the management. Of the many rows, two of the most memorable centred around plays by Sean O'Casey (1880–1964). In 1926 his *The Plough and The Stars* led to riots by patriots

RIGHT *Mrs Patrick Campbell as
Deirdre in J.M. Synge's* Deirdre
of the Sorrows *at the Abbey
Theatre.*

BELOW *Irish piper's costume
designed by Eamonn Ceannt for his
London concert in 1903, and worn
when he played Irish pipes before
Pope Pius X in the Vatican in
1908. Ceannt, a Commandant in
the 1916 Rising, was executed at
Kilmainham Jail that year.*

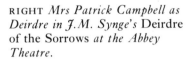

who considered that he had denigrated the heroes of the 1916 Easter Rising, and
his Expressionist anti-war drama *The Silver Tassie* was rejected by the Abbey
management for fear of a similar reaction. It may be hard for us now to imagine
that Synge's *The Shadow of the Glen* caused an uproar, but it was branded as offen-
sive to the (recently created) image of chaste Irish womanhood. The hard-line Irish
nationalists were incensed also by Synge's interpretation of the violence, decadence
and frustration of Irish life in *The Playboy of the Western World*. Synge shared
Augusta Gregory's aristocratic Protestant landlord background, and her deep and
real understanding of rural Ireland, of peasant life and lore and of the Irish language.

Nationalists who cherished an image of viceless Irish peasantry would not admit
to any flaws in the national character, past or present; to them all evil came from
an alien source. Side by side with the outwardly circumspect and moralizing society
of Victorian England, based on models of Protestant puritanism, the new Roman
Catholic bourgeoisie in Victorian Ireland revered Celtic Christian Ireland as a model
of morality, chastity, scholarship, asceticism and piety. In their adulation of the
saints and scholars they ignored the quite extraordinary aberrations of the early
church. Few people in Ireland would have been unwise enough to risk a riot by
levelling any criticism at the hallowed heroes and saintly monks. When Standish
O'Grady presented the Celtic heroic cycles to a nineteenth-century public he ex-
purgated the lusty, the bawdy, and the coarse. The nineteenth-century Roman
Catholic Church, emerging triumphantly from centuries of suppression in Ireland,
effectively put her stamp of propriety not only on contemporary society but also
on the nation's past and inevitably its future.

George Moore strongly resented what he considered the hypocrisy of the prevailing piety, and came to believe that what he felt to be the overbearing influence of
the Roman Catholic Church hampered artistic and cultural awakening. A Catholic
himself, he converted to the Church of Ireland in order to register his disapproval

of Irish Roman Catholicism in a situation where he sensed the necessity of being one or the other. His *A Drama in Muslin* is a merciless portrayal of rural and urban Ireland of the 1880s, revealing the threadbare misery of the poor and the shallow pageantry of the gentry from which he himself sprang. In a later novel, *The Lake*, he described the agony and frustration of a country priest who makes a bid for freedom.

Moore spent much of his life in voluntary exile in London. James Joyce, who became known in Dublin literary circles in 1902 and was to overshadow all the stars in the Irish literary firmament, left Ireland in 1904 to live and write abroad, attracted by Continental literary trends and fearful of parochialism and provincialism in the literary movement of his native country. Unlike two of his most famous literary compatriots, George Bernard Shaw and Oscar Wilde, who both lived in England, Joyce, working in voluntary exile, chose Dublin and the pathos of life in Ireland as the central theme for his work; it can safely be said that no writer has ever given the Irish scene richer, fuller or more incisive expression.

Crafts

Ireland's Industrial Exhibition of 1852 and subsequent exhibitions stimulated the production of jewellery, furniture and bric à brac, much of which reflected the current interest in the ancient national past. Copies of ancient fibulae and brooches were made, as well as pieces whose design was based freely on early originals. These revival objects excited even more popular interest after the discovery of the Tara Brooch. The designers and artisans also worked from the repertoire of national emblems; the shamrock, the harp, the wolfhound, the figure of Hibernia, and the round tower all appeared in silverware, glassware and Belleek china, in woodcarving and on shopfronts and tombstones.

One of the banners designed by Jack Yeats for Loughrea Cathedral, County Galway – St Patrick banishing the snakes.

Edward Martyn of Tullira, an aesthete whose interests ranged from literature and drama to the reform of church music, was instrumental in founding a stained glass workshop in Ireland. The windows of the many nineteenth-century Roman Catholic churches were glazed with imported stained glass, mostly from the Continent, from the firm of Mayer in Munich. Edward Martyn brought an English stained glass artist, A.E. Childe, to Ireland, and encouraged the painter Sarah Purser to set up a workshop in Dublin in 1903; it was called An Tur Gloine (the Glass Tower) and there, under Childe's direction, the art was taught and developed. Many talented artists emerged from this studio, not least Sarah Purser herself, Michael Healy and Wilhelmina Geddes, but the best-known must be Evie Hone (1894–1935). Harry Clarke (1899–1931), who must rank as one of the most brilliant stained glass artists, was a contemporary of the younger members of An Tur Gloine, but not one of the group. In the Dun Emer workshops of Evelyn Gleeson, tapestries, banners and liturgical vestments of great beauty were embroidered, many of them with designs from Celtic Christian art. This Celtic Revival work could easily have been blandly derivative, but is instead, at its best, vigorous, appealing and imaginative, especially where artists have applied ancient ornamentation to new media.

The language revival

Douglas Hyde (1860–1949), whose background of Anglo-Irish Protestant gentry and clergy was similar to that of Yeats, and who was a friend and 'folkloring' companion of Augusta Gregory, patronized a literary movement parallel to that of Yeats, but divergent in that it rejected the English language as an acceptable vehicle for an Irish national literature. Hyde, brought up in County Roscommon, believed passionately that the Celtic heritage could only survive and be preserved in the Irish language, and that Irish as a national language was essential to the recovery and establishment of a national identity. He therefore preached the necessity of de-Anglicizing Ireland. This call fell on the willing ears of those heirs of Young Irelandism who were cultural separatists, with a vision restricted to black-and-white terms – all good equals Ireland, all bad equals England. Hyde became the first president of the Gaelic League, founded in 1893 to arrest the decline of spoken Irish and promote a nationwide revival of the Irish language. Hyde wanted the League to be a non-political movement which would unite all the partisans of Irish culture, but it naturally attracted political nationalists and they in fact outnumbered the purely cultural nationalists. Gaelic enthusiasts attempted a revival of ancient costume; Lord Ashbourne, an Anglo-Irish Protestant peer who supported the cause, addressed the House of Lords in London in Irish and wore a green and saffron kilt. Simultaneously the Gaelic League, and other societies such as the Gaelic Athletic Association, stimulated the recovery of separatist nationalism and the revival of the Irish Republican Brotherhood.

Revolutionary nationalism

Veterans of a small, unsuccessful rising in 1848, some of whom had fled to the United States, founded the Irish Republican Brotherhood there and in Ireland. This was a secret society, also known as the Fenians, whose members were bound by oath to its aim of armed revolution. Among the Irish working in America, nursing bitter memories of the famine and social injustice, the Fenians gained support and finance. By 1865, within less than 10 years of its foundation, the movement had enrolled a staggering 80,000 members from Irish in their own country and in Britain. Henceforth the nationalism camp was divided between supporters of moderate Catholic nationalism, including a few Protestant nationalists, and the radical, revolutionary, social nationalism of the Fenians, essentially working-class and in communion with Continental European revolutionaries through their chief organizer, James Stephens. The Fenian rebellion of 1867 was quashed by the government and harsh sentences imposed on its leaders, but the spirit of Fenianism survived this setback. The heirs of the Fenians played a central role half a century later in the rebellion of 1916; now, more than a century after the failure of the 1867 rebellion, the revolutionary political legacy of the Irish Republican Brotherhood is shared by groups dedicated to violent confrontation with the British government in Northern Ireland.

Reforms The disestablishment of the Church of Ireland in 1869 and the Land Act of 1870 were judicious moves by Gladstone's government to take the heat out of the Irish situation; they had the affect of sweetening the moderate Roman Catholics and their hierarchy and reducing agrarian discontent. But the land reforms were inadequate and the demand for fair rents and security of tenure burgeoned from sporadic acts of local agitation into the formation of the Land League, in which some Fenians – principally Michael Davitt – played an active part. The agitation organized by the Land League between 1879 and 1882 is remembered as the 'Land War'.

One Member of Parliament, Charles Stewart Parnell, a Protestant Anglo-Irish landowner from County Wicklow, took up the cause of the agitators for land reforms. Despite his background he won the sympathy of the Fenians, and his prestige among Irish nationalists was enhanced when he and other Irish MPs were gaoled for causing disorder in the House of Commons. As a result of the efforts of Parnell and his supporters the Land Act of 1881 was passed, providing for the establishment of a fair rent tribunal. Subsequent acts of 1885 and 1903 (the Wyndham Act) paved the way for the completion of a social revolution in the ownership and distribution of land; this they did by pushing landlords to sell and assisting tenant farmers to buy, so that by 1917 two out of every three farmers in Ireland owned their own farm and land. The establishment in 1891 of another body, the Congested Districts Board, created to provide government aid in the underprivileged, distressed regions of western Ireland, stimulated agriculture, cottage industry and land reclamation.

Unfortunately, by the time help reached rural Ireland large numbers of landless, unemployed country people had flocked into the cities, especially Dublin, creating some of the most appalling slum conditions in Europe, with overcrowded, unhygienic tenements which were breeding grounds of righteous discontent. It is not surprising,

The British lion draws blood in a cartoon from the supplement to the Freeman's Weekly. *The 'Children of Erin' ask, 'Oh, Mother! Has that animal gone mad?' Erin answers: 'Yes, my dear children. He is in one of his periodical Anti-Irish frenzies....'*

A view of Victorian artisan dwellings at Cobh, County Cork, one of the towns whose population mushroomed in the period of urban growth.

therefore, that a powerful trade union movement grew rapidly under the charismatic leadership of James Larkin, and that his successor James Connolly, who had founded the Irish Socialist Republican party in 1896, was able to found a workers' force, the Irish Citizen Army, which aimed to establish a workers' republic.

The Home Rule *movement* Moderate nationalists, the political heirs of O'Connell's Repeal Association, dissatisfied with the policy of the government, revived the principle of an Irish legislative body in Dublin. Parnell, who supported this policy, made the movement for Home Rule into a tremendous political force, attractive to all but the most extreme Fenians. It was approved by the now powerful Roman Catholic hierarchy, which was bitterly opposed to the revolutionary socialism of Fenianism. In the general election of 1885 the Irish Home Rule party, led by Parnell, won 85 Irish seats; it was thus in a position to hold the balance of power in the House of Commons by supporting either the Conservatives or the Liberals. Shrewdly, Gladstone's Liberal party adopted the cause of Irish Home Rule to win the support of the 85 Irish MPs, but his decision split his party. A first Irish Home Rule Bill of 1886 was defeated, as was a second in 1893. Unfortunately, Parnell's involvement in a divorce action in 1890 prompted the Roman Catholic hierarchy to withdraw their support from him; internal feuds in the Home Rule party ensued. Parnell lost the support of the majority and died in 1891.

After being weakened and rent by factions the party began to recover 10 years later under the leadership of John Redmond. The reduction of the Liberal majority in 1910 once again put the balance of power in the hands of the Irish Home Rule

MPs, so that the third Home Rule Bill was passed by the Commons in 1912. Most Protestants in Ireland, and particularly the compact Protestant community in Ulster, were strongly opposed to Home Rule; it would have put paid to their privileged position and made them a minority group in an overwhelmingly Roman Catholic Ireland, whose cultural, social, religious, and linguistic heritage they rejected as alien to their own.

Carson, the Unionist leader, established a para-military force to resist Home Rule in Ulster. As a counter measure, the Irish Volunteer Force of 100,000 men was founded in the south, and, to the alarm of constitutional Home Rule leaders, was soon infiltrated by revolutionary Fenian activists. Both forces imported armaments. The Fenians too were arming and reorganizing; the workers' Irish Citizen Army was seething with resentment and a desire for action. The official British Army was the fifth force in this tense situation. When the Irish Home Rule Bill was placed on the statute book in 1914 it included a proviso to placate Carson's militant Unionists, allowing them to opt out for a period. However, the outbreak of the World War in the summer of 1914 caused the implementation of Home Rule to be suspended for its duration. Many Ulster Volunteers went into the British Army to fight against Germany. Redmond urged the Irish Volunteers to do so too. The IVF split, the majority remaining loyal to Redmond and the British cause in the war, and a minority of about 10,000, with strong republican sympathies, seceded.

The Easter Rising   The secessionist Irish Volunteers (led by Pádraic Pearse and Eoin Mac Neill), the Irish Republican Brotherhood and the Irish Citizen Army raised an insurrection

149

in Dublin in Easter week, 1916. The rising was put down within a week, its failure caused by a number of factors ranging from the non-arrival of promised help, in the form of arms, from Germany, the lack of co-ordination at command level between the various bands of insurgents, and the failure of massive popular support from the population, many of whom had sons, husbands and brothers in the British Army fighting against Germany. In the seventeenth century the Irish had looked to Spain for help, in the eighteenth century to France, and in the twentieth century to Germany. These enemies of England and would-be allies of Ireland all proved slow to render effective help, or to launch a full attack on England through Ireland, but to the English these incidents only confirmed their belief in the unreliable and treacherous nature of the Irish. After the suppression of the Easter Rising the government could have gained support and favour among the Irish at large, many of whom, moderate nationalists, were actually hostile to the revolutionaries. Instead, the authorities committed the error of adopting the harshest possible attitude to the rebels, believing that it would put an end to their cause. The execution of the leaders and the prison sentences imposed turned the tide of Irish public opinion implacably against England. The rebel leaders became national heroes. The Sinn Fein party, founded by Arthur Griffith in 1905 to propose a dual monarchy system as an alternative to Home Rule, was transformed into a republican political separatist movement which, in the first post-war elections of 1918, swept the country, crushing the Home Rulers by winning 73 seats.

The names of the parties and organized groups, the dates, the number of their adherents – these facts of history spelt out for the next generation a deeply troubled situation at a human level: friends and families were divided and the national consciousness riven by the complications of conflicting religious, social and political loyalties, the ties of ancestry, tradition and sentiment, and the dictates of duty, creed, honour, gratitude, anger, fear, frustration and resentment.

Independence

The elected Sinn Fein MPs decided to boycott the parliament to which they had been elected. They gathered in Dublin in January 1919, and unilaterally declared themselves the national parliament of Ireland. They confirmed the proclamation, made by Pádraic Pearse at the Easter 1916 rebellion, of the Irish Republic as a sovereign state, and constituted a provisional government; Eamon de Valera, born in New York City of a Cuban father and an Irish emigrant mother, became the president. This provisional government was not recognized by the British government, whose efforts to suppress it led to fighting between the police and the British troops on one side, and the supporters of de Valera's government under the command of Michael Collins and Cathal Brugha on the other; the Irish Volunteers were then increasingly referred to as the Irish Republican Army. The shootings, the burning of houses, the acts of cruelty perpetrated at the expense of the populace by undisciplined British soldiers, the hated Black and Tans, and the romantic appeal of the republican fighting an overwhelming enemy, all combined to win over moderate nationalist feeling to the republican side. Meanwhile in Ulster there was an outbreak of political and sectarian violence.

The Government of Ireland Act, passed by the British Parliament in 1920, provided for two separate Home Rule systems in Ireland, each with its own parliamentary machinery – one in Belfast with jurisdiction over six of the nine counties of Ulster in the north-east, and one in Dublin with jurisdiction over the remaining 26 counties. Peace negotiations between de Valera's provisional government and the British government began after a truce was declared to halt fighting in the War of Independence in July 1921; in December of that year a treaty was signed which provided for the establishment of an Irish Free State with the status of a Dominion

OPPOSITE ABOVE *The ancient Gaelic game of hurling is still very popular; Cork and Kilkenny fight it out during the All-Ireland Minor Final at Croke Park, Dublin.*

OPPOSITE BELOW LEFT *In spite of Oscar Wilde's caustic judgment, 'the unspeakable in full pursuit of the uneatable', fox-hunting is still a popular sport in a country that abounds in suitable open countryside.*

OPPOSITE BELOW RIGHT *A view of the new Goff's Bloodstock Sales Complex, the work of the architects Scott, Tallon and Walker.*

in the British Commonwealth, and contained a proviso allowing the northern parliament to opt out by vote, a prerogative which they exercised at once.

The terms of the treaty fell short of the aims of the republicans. The majority in the government agreed to accept them as better than nothing and as a stepping stone to attain the degree of independence they really wanted. A large faction, however, led by de Valera, refused to accept the treaty. This led to the outbreak of the grim Civil War between Free-Staters and anti-Free-Staters which further shocked and rent the already sadly fragmented country and took a further toll of lives, among them Cathal Brugha and Michael Collins, the Free-State leader. Before the war ended with the capitulation of de Valera's anti-Free-Staters in May 1923, Ireland had lost its precious national archives in the shelling of the Dublin Four Courts, many country houses had been burned to the ground and a number of people had turned their backs in despair on the strife-ridden country.

In 1926 de Valera formed his followers into a political party, Fianna Fail, which, when it came to power in the elections of 1932, abolished the oath of allegiance to the British crown. By referendum in 1937 a new constitution was adopted which declared Ireland to be a 'sovereign, independent, democratic state'; Douglas Hyde came out of retirement to become its first president in 1938. The description of the 26-county state was changed to the Republic of Ireland in 1949, and Ireland seceded from the Commonwealth. By a startlingly large majority of 83 per cent, the citizens of the Republic of Ireland voted in 1972 to enter the European Economic Community.

The young republic, which has the fastest growing economy of any of the countries in the community, faces many challenges – economic, social, political, religious and cultural – and not least the attitude to partition and guerrilla warfare in Northern Ireland. Now, freed from the restricting shackles of both oppression and narrow nationalism, the Irish can truly establish their identity. How they will do so and what it will be, the future will show. That there is no lack of artistic talent we may be sure, but despite the government's provisions to attract writers and artists to live and work in Ireland, two of the best known in the field of letters – Samuel Beckett and the novelist Edna O'Brien – live abroad as expatriates. On the other hand contemporary poets living and working in Ireland have achieved and are achieving international recognition, worthily upholding Ireland's centuries-long tradition in this field. In spite of the more alluring financial opportunities abroad, some good actors and actresses have chosen to remain in Dublin, and it maintains its theatrical reputation. After a period when little could be built because of the depressed economic situation, architects in Ireland are rising to meet the need for new churches, factories and public buildings. Irish musical groups like The Planxty, The Wild Geese and The Chieftains are acclaimed in many countries for their performances of Gaelic folk music in a modern idiom, in which traditional instruments are used. The Irish equestrian world is flourishing; breeding, racing and hunting, for which the Irish countryside is particularly suitable, are as popular as ever. The ancient Gaelic game of hurling is now a national sport. The Irish language is alive and well. So, like Oisín Kelly's wondering figures, we can gaze admiringly at the new, and ponder Ireland's complex, often sad, but unique and infinitely rich legacies from the past.

A sculpture by Oisín Kelly outside the new County Hall, Cork.

BELOW *Completed in 1970 by Ronald Tallon of Scott, Tallon and Walker, the Carroll Factory at Dundalk, County Louth, has a reflecting pool and sculpture by Gerda Frömel. The complex shows a beauty rarely found in industrial buildings.*

Glossary

Alumnus Pupil of a school or university.

Aniconic Not having the nature of a portrait.

Antae In this instance refers to projections of the north and south walls of a church building jutting beyond the east wall.

Arris Moulding Moulding with a sharp edge formed by the meeting of two surfaces.

Asvamehda Vedic rite in Ancient India in which the monarch sacrificed a horse to celebrate his own paramountcy.

Cable Moulding Convex moulding resembling a rope.

Caput Chief place, capital.

Coenobitic Pertaining to a resident monastic community.

Colobium Long tunic, usually sleeveless, but occasionally with short sleeves.

Corbelled Built with a series of courses, each projecting beyond the one below it to form a support.

Cottier Peasant renting a smallholding under a system of land tenure whereby the land was let annually in small plots directly to the labourers.

Currach Coracle-type boat made of wickerwork covered with hides.

En échelon Projecting forward in parallel lines facing one another.

Fibula Buckle.

Flabella Plural of flabellum – a fan used in religious ceremonies.

Fosterage System by which children were entrusted to a foster-mother.

Glibes Forelocks worn by the Irish.

Glossed With explanatory renderings added to the text.

Glossography The writing or compiling of an explanatory commentary or gloss.

Hagiography Biography of a saint.

Half-uncials Letters of a distinctive style of script in which miniscule forms were mixed with standard uncial writing.

Hegemony Predominance of one group over others.

Honour-price The amount due to a person under the Brehon Laws in compensation for an offence committed against him. It varied according to rank or occupation.

Iconic Of the nature of a portrait.

Justiciary The chief political and judicial officer in the Anglo-Norman and Plantagenet administration in Ireland who acted as regent in the absence of the monarch.

Kern Lightly-armed Irish foot-soldier.

Majuscule The equivalent, in modern typographical terms, of upper case.

Mensa In this instance refers to the table-like slab on top of a sarcophagus.

Minuscule The equivalent, in modern typographical terms, of lower case.

Miscegenation Mixture of races.

Mural Stair Steps built into a wall.

Niello A black composition of metallic alloys used for filling in engraved designs on silver and other metals.

Peter's Pence An annual tax (originally one penny from each householder of a certain substance) paid to the Holy See. The term now applies to voluntary contributions to the patrimony of the Holy See.

Piscina A shallow basin with a drain in which the altar vessels are washed.

Scriptoria Plural of scriptorium – the writing-room of the monastery where manuscripts were prepared and copied.

Sedilia A series of seats (often three – for the priest, deacon and sub-deacon) in the south wall of the chancel.

Senachies Professional story-tellers.

Slype Covered passage leading east from the cloister.

Solifluction The flow of water-saturated soil down a steep slope.

Tanistry The system of succession whereby an estate or dignity passed to one of the kin of the deceased, chosen as the worthiest by the other members of the clan or extended family. The heir apparent thus chosen was called the tanist.

Tympanum In this instance the space above the lintel of the doorway and below the arch above it.

Ultramontane Term used to describe persons or parties distinguished by their zeal for Papal authority and their support for the doctrine of absolute Papal supremacy.

Voussoir A wedge-shaped stone which forms one of the units of an arch.

Further Reading

Craig, M., and The Knight of Glin, *Ireland Observed*, Cork, 1970
Crookshank, A., and The Knight of Glin, *The Painters of Ireland, c. 1660-1920*, London, 1978
de Breffny, B., *Castles of Ireland*, London and New York, 1977
de Breffny, B., ed., *The Irish World*, London and New York, 1977
de Breffny, B., *The Land of Ireland*, London and New York, 1979
de Breffny, B., and R. ffolliott, *The Houses of Ireland*, London and New York, 1975
de Breffny, B., and G. Mott, *The Churches and Abbeys of Ireland*, London and New York, 1976
Evans, E.E., *Prehistoric and Early Christian Ireland*, London and New York, 1966
Evans, E.E., *The Personality of Ireland: Habitat, Heritage and History*, Cambridge, 1973
Guinness, D., and W. Ryan, *Irish Houses and Castles*, London, 1971
Harbison, P., *The Archaeology of Ireland*, London and New York, 1976
Harbison, P., Potterton, H., and J. Sheehy, *Irish Art and Architecture*, London and New York, 1978
Henry, F. *Irish Art in the Romanesque Period, 1020–1120 AD*, London and New York, 1970
Herity, M., and G. Eogan, *Ireland in Prehistory*, London and Boston, 1970
Sheehy, J., *Discovering Ireland's Past, The Celtic Revival*, London, 1979
Stalley, R.A., *Architecture and Sculpture in Ireland, 1150–1350*, Dublin, 1970

Acknowledgments

The author wishes to thank all the archives and institutions who kindly answered requests for illustrations or who gave permission for photography, and the people who helped by procuring and loaning photographs for the book, in particular Professor Anne O. Crookshank, Department of Visual Arts, Trinity College, Dublin, and also Miss Rosemary ffolliott, the Hon. Desmond Guinness and Mr Sean Rafferty. Mr Philip MacDonagh, then of the Embassy of Ireland, Rome, was helpful over the difficulties occasioned by the postal strike in the Republic of Ireland. The majority of objects in the National Museum of Ireland were photographed by Mr Brendan Doyle, whose friendly and efficient co-operation is greatly appreciated. Judy Allen typed the text.

Most of the colour and black-and-white illustrations were photographed by George Mott, who also undertook the picture research. The remaining illustrations were provided by the following sources. Numbers in *italics* indicate colour pages.

Abbey Theatre, Dublin: 144 above
Ashmolean Museum, Oxford: 80
Bord Failte, London: 40, 151 below left, 151 above, endpapers
British Museum, London: 52
City of Manchester Art Gallery: 141
Commissioners of Public Works, Dublin: 14 right, 16 (photographs by Jim Bambury)
Country Life, London: 113
Courtauld Institute of Art, London: 95
Professor Anne O. Crookshank: 70 left (photograph by Jonathan Harsch)
Wendy Dallas: *98, 134–5*
Department of the Environment (Northern Ireland), Belfast: 24 right
John Donat: 151 below right, 153 above
Miss Rosemary ffolliott: 120 left (photograph by Gordon Ledbetter)
Field Museum of Natural History, Chicago: 10
Jonathan Harsch: 139 below
Hermitage Museum, Leningrad: 106
The Irish Ancestor, Dublin, by courtesy of Miss M.P. Ringwood: 120 right
Irish Franciscan College, Rome, by courtesy of the Rector: 101, 122 left
    (photographs by George Mott)
Musée de Versailles: 107 above left
National Library of Ireland, Dublin: 112 below, 119
National Museum of Ireland, Dublin: 14 left, 18, 19, 20, 23 right, 24 left, *26, 27 below*, 38, 39, 41,
    42 below, 42 right, 44, 45, 72, 121 centre, 121 right, 144 below
Österreichische Nationalbibliothek, Vienna: 107 below left, 107 above right
Radio Times Hulton Picture Library, London: 142 left, 142 right, 143 left, 143 right
Sheffield City Art Galleries: 128, 131
The Hon. Guy Strutt: 138
Trinity College, Dublin: *25*
Universidad de Chile, Santiago: 107 below right
Weidenfeld and Nicolson Archive: 94 left, 94 right

Maps on p. 15 after *Ireland in Prehistory* by M. Herity and G. Eogan, by courtesy of the authors.
Maps drawn by John Gilkes

Index

Numbers in *italics* refer to illustrations